The Road of Lost Innocence

SOMALY MAM

with Ruth Marshall

Spiegel & Grau

NEW YORK . 2009

2009 Spiegel & Grau Trade Paperback Edition

Library of Congress Cataloging-in-Publication Data
Mam, Somaly.
[Silence de l'innocence. English]
The road of lost innocence / by Somaly Mam with Ruth Marshall.—1st ed.
p. cm.
ISBN 978-0-385-52622-7
1. Child prostitution—Cambodia. 2. Child sexual abuse—Cambodia.
3. Children—Crimes against—Cambodia. 4. Mam, Somaly. 5. Afesip
(Organization) I. Marshall, Ruth, 1961–ƒ II. Title.
HQ242.3.A5M3613 2008
362.76092—dc22
[B]
2008028302

Book design by Jennifer Ann Daddio

By far the lowest statistic for the number of prostitutes
and sex slaves in Cambodia is between 40,000 and 50,000.
It can be expected that at least 1 in 40 girls born in
Cambodia will be sold into sex slavery.

—2005 report by Future Group,
a Canadian nongovernmental organization

In 1986, when I was sold to a brothel as a prostitute, I was about sixteen years old. Today there are many far younger prostitutes in Cambodia. There are virgins for sale in every large town, and to ensure their virginity, the girls are sometimes as young as five or six.

In Cambodia, and throughout Southeast Asia, tens of thousands of minor children are forced into prostitution annually. They are raped and beaten, often for years. Many are killed.

I dedicate this book to the thousands of little girls who are sold into prostitution every year.

Contents

Foreword by Nicholas D. Kristof

When I made my first reporting trips to Cambodia's brothels, more than a dozen years ago, I was completely unprepared for the sights I encountered. My first stop was the Svay Pak brothel district, notorious for selling girls as young as five or six. The pimps weren't concerned about getting in trouble, so I was able to walk from brothel to brothel, interviewing girls imprisoned there. Some were virgins, awaiting sale, and they were particularly haggard and terrified.

The next day I visited the Tuol Kok district in the capital of Phnom Penh and spent the afternoon interviewing two girls imprisoned in one brothel. One was fourteen and had been sold by her stepfather; the other was fifteen and had been kidnapped and sold. They were best friends and tried to cheer each other up, but they had no ray of hope in their lives. A week earlier, the mother of the fifteen-year-old had found her daughter, after searching all over Cambodia following her disappearance. But the brothel owner refused to give the girl back to her mother, saying, "She's mine. I paid good money for her. You can buy her back."

The brothel next door had burned down recently, and the corpses of two girls had been found afterward in the charred ruins. They had been chained up because the owner thought they might try to run away. Likewise, these two girls I was interviewing were never allowed out; their only escape would be to die of AIDS. If they managed to flee the building, the police would chase them down and return them to the brothel, where they would face severe beatings or electric shocks. There was no way to help them, and I left the brothel knowing that I had a good front-page story, but also feeling that I had been one more person coming through, taking advantage of these two girls. More broadly, I left Cambodia staggered by what I had seen: this wasn't what Americans thought of as prostitution. This was what Americans thought of as slavery. The biggest difference from nineteenth-century slavery was that these girls were likely to be dead of AIDS by their twenties.

Since that first trip, I've returned repeatedly to report on human trafficking in Cambodia and have written widely on the problem in other countries as well. There's growing recognition that trafficking is one of the great human rights injustices of the twenty-first century and that more women and girls are now trafficked into slavery annually than slaves were transported to the New World at the peak of the transatlantic slave trade. In the course of my reporting, I came to know Somaly Mam, who was enslaved herself but managed to escape—and then became the Harriet Tubman of Southeast Asia's brothels, repeatedly rescuing those left behind. As a local person with firsthand experience in the red-light districts, Somaly has a credibility and understanding that no outsider does, and the rescued girls adore her and treat her as a mother. She teases them and scolds them to make them laugh; she tells them that they're pretty; she showers them in love. One girl she had rescued had had her eye gouged out by a brothel owner, and Somaly hugged her as she wept but then told her how lovely she would look with the glass eye being arranged for her and talked about how she would get married—and soon the girl was laughing as well as weeping.

I've seen Somaly honored in America, and she wows the audiences as she speaks in English—her fourth language, not bad for a woman who never got an education—but I doubt that those audiences truly can appreciate the danger that she faces. When the spotlights fade and the applause dies, Somaly goes right back out to the red-light districts where the pimps want to kill her. She has had a gun held to her head, she's been threatened repeatedly, and when none of that worked, the pimps tried to intimidate her by kidnapping her daughter. Yet Somaly is one of the most stubborn people I know, and she just will not quit.

It has made a difference. Because of her work and that of many others in Cambodia, some of the worst abuses have been curbed. The Svay Pak brothels no longer openly display young girls, and some pimps have gone to prison for selling virgins. You see fewer twelve- and thirteen-year-old girls in the brothels today; rather, there are sixteen-year-olds who claim to be eighteen. Some brothels have closed, because the owners find it's not worth the risk of prosecution and the hassle of raids. It's not a solution, but it is progress.

This is Somaly's story, and she is an extraordinary guide through a netherworld few outsiders can imagine. But remember, too, that hers is a hopeful story. She may describe killings and torture, but the larger story is of triumph, love, and rehabilitation. Her centers for rescued girls are hopeful, not depressing, and Somaly herself is a tribute to the resilience, courage, and nobility of the human spirit.

NICHOLAS KRISTOF
March 2009

Introduction

This could be a tragic story, and of course it is.

However, to me it is also—and maybe most of all—the inspiring and beautiful story of one woman's courage.

Every day around the world, women and children are sold into prostitution. It is a modern version of slavery, and it is as ugly as slavery has always been.

Somaly Mam's raw autobiography takes place mainly in Cambodia, but human trafficking, rape, murder, and the violent exploitation of women and children is happening all over the world. It's happening in the West, and yes, it's happening in your own state.

You and I may choose to turn a blind eye, but this does not alter the ugly reality.

It is impossible to know exactly how many people are

being sold and forced into prostitution every year, but the numbers cited in a comprehensive UN report from February 2009 on human trafficking are staggering, and they serve as terrifying testimony to the general lack of legal action and implementation of humanitarian laws that already exist in countries all over the world.

Most victims of trafficking are victims of sexual exploitation. Most of them are women, and many of them are children.

Some are sold into prostitution by their own parents, sisters, brothers, grandparents, aunts, or uncles. Some are lured away from their families on the pretext of a much-needed job elsewhere. And some are simply kidnapped. Their fate is all the same: they are sold as mere livestock and treated worse than animals.

We may choose to ignore this global tragedy, this brutal, ongoing crime. As for Somaly Mam, she does not have a choice. She cannot pretend that women and children are not sold, terrorized, and murdered every day around the world. Because she knows. Her sleepless nights and the scars she bears on her body serve as haunting reminders.

She works tirelessly to save as many victims of abuse and trafficking as she can, but she cannot do it alone. She needs us to change our way of thinking. She needs us to change the mentality of our boys and men so they no longer find it natural to mistreat and abuse women and children for their own pleasure. She needs women to look differently upon those who represent what they themselves could have been. She needs governments to enforce the laws that have already been created. And she needs us all to speak up for those who cannot speak for themselves. Because they have to keep silent to survive, because they may not know that they have rights—or because it is already too late.

For years, silence equaled survival for Somaly Mam. Now her hard-earned courage to speak out is saving thousands of others who have had their lives destroyed. Toward this end, she has written this personal, raw, and uputdownable book, which you will read with a lump in your throat.

Somaly Mam's story is an account of the lowest kind of human depravity, but it is also a testimony to resistance, and to hope. She lifted herself out of a well of terror and found the determination and the resilience to save others.

Somaly Mam is my candidate for the Nobel Peace Prize. She is living proof that one woman *can* change the fate of others.

So can you.

AYAAN HIRSI ALI
February 2009

The Forest

My name is Somaly. At least that's the name I have now. Like everyone in Cambodia, I've had several. Names are the result of temporary choices. You change them the way you'd change lives. As a small child, I was called Ya, and sometimes just Non—"Little One." When I was taken away from the forest by the old man, I was called Aya, and once, at a border crossing, he told the guard my name was Viriya—I don't really know why. I got used to people calling me all sorts of names, mostly insults. Then, years later, a kind man who said he was my uncle gave me the name Somaly: "The Necklace of Flowers Lost in the Virgin Forest." I liked it; it seemed to fit the idea of who I felt I really was. When I finally had the choice, I decided to keep that name as my own.

I will never know what my parents called me. But then I

have nothing from them, no memories at all. My adoptive father once gave me this typically Khmer advice: "You shouldn't try to discover the past. You shouldn't hurt yourself." I suspect he knows what really happened, but he has never talked to me about it. The little I do know I've had to piece together with vague recollections and some help from history.

I spent my earliest years in the rolling countryside of northeastern Cambodia, surrounded by savanna and forests, not far from the high plains of Vietnam. Even today, when I have the chance to go into the forest, I feel at home. I recognize smells. I recognize plants. I instinctively know what's good to eat and what's poisonous. I remember the waterfalls. The sound of them is still in my ears. We children would bathe naked under the cascading water and play at holding our breath. I remember the smell of the virgin forest. I have a buried memory of this place.

The people of Bou Sra, the village where I was born, are Phnong. They are an old tribe of mountain people, quite unlike the Khmer who dominate the lowlands of Cambodia. I have inherited the typical Phnong dark skin from my mother. Cambodians see it as black and ugly. In Khmer, the word "Phnong" means "savage." Throughout Southeast Asia, people are very sensitive about skin color. The paler you are, the closer to "moon color," the more highly you are prized. A plump woman with white skin is the supreme object of beauty and desire. I was dark and thin and very unattractive.

I was born sometime around 1970 or 1971, when the Troubles began in Cambodia. My parents left me with my maternal grandmother when I was still a small child. Perhaps they were seeking a better life, or perhaps they were forced to leave. Before I turned five, the country had been carpet-bombed by the Americans. Then it was seized by the murderous regime of Pol Pot's Khmer Rouge. The four years of Khmer Rouge rule, from 1975 to 1979, were responsible for the deaths of about one in five people in Cambodia through execution, starvation, or forced labor. In the storm of events, countless others were simply swept away from their villages and families without leaving a trace. People were displaced to work camps, where they toiled as slaves, or were forced to fight for the regime. There are many reasons why my parents might have left the forest.

The story I like to tell myself is that my parents and grandmother always had my best interests at heart. Among the Phnong, the mother's lineage determines ethnicity. So despite my father being Khmer, when my parents left, my place was with the Phnong in Mondulkiri Province. Not long thereafter my grandmother would also disappear, much too soon for me to have any lasting memory of her. Mountain people up and leave for any old reason, as soon as anything displeases them. No one expected an explanation, especially not during those troubled years. So when my grandmother left the forest, no one knew where she went. I don't think I was abandoned—she probably thought I'd be safest in the village. There was no way she could have known that the forest would not be my home for long.

Our village was nothing more than a dozen round huts clustered in a forest clearing. The huts were made of plaited bamboo, their straw roofs low to the ground. Most families shared a single large hut with no partition between the communal sleeping platform and the cooking area. Other families kept themselves separate. With no parents or other family in the village, I would sleep on my own in a hammock. I lived like a little savage. I slept here or there, and ate where I could. I was at home everywhere and nowhere. I don't remember any other children who slept alone among the trees, as I did. Perhaps I wasn't taken in by anyone because I was of mixed race—part Phnong and part Khmer. Or perhaps I just made a decision to be by myself. Being an orphan in Cambodia is no rare condition. It is frighteningly ordinary.

I wasn't generally unhappy, but I remember feeling cold all the time. On particularly bitter or rainy nights, a kind man, Taman, would make space for me in his home. He was a Cham, a Muslim Khmer, but his wife was Phnong. I can't remember her name, but I thought she was beautiful with her long black hair tied behind her head with a bamboo stick, her high cheekbones, and a necklace made of shiny black wood and animal teeth. She was nice to me. Sometimes she would try to wash my long hair, rubbing the ash of a special herb into it to clean it, and then oiling it with pig fat and combing it with her fingers while she sang. She wore an intricately woven black and red cloth around her waist. Some women would leave their breasts bare, but Taman's wife covered hers.

Taman, like the other men, wore a loincloth that left his buttocks bare. The men wore strings of beads and bows strapped to their backs and had thick cylinders of wood pierced through their earlobes.

We children would be naked most of the time. We would play or help make clothes together out of thick, flat leaves wrapped with vines. Taman's wife would weave for hours on end, sitting on the floor with her legs stretched out in front of her and the bamboo loom tied to her feet.

Her teeth were filed into sharp points. Phnong girls file

and blacken their teeth when they become women, but I left the village long before the time for filing teeth.

I was always looking for a mother so that I could be held in her arms, kissed, and stroked, like Taman's wife held her children. I was very unhappy not to have a mother like everyone else. My only confidants were the trees. I talked to them and told them about my sorrow. They listened, understood, and made discreet signs in my direction. They were my only true friends, along with the moon. When things got unbearable, I confessed my secrets to the waterfalls, because the water couldn't reverse its flow and betray me. Even today, I sometimes talk to trees. Other than that, I almost never spoke as a child. There wouldn't have been much point—nobody would have listened.

I found my own food. I would roam the forest and eat what I could find: fruit, wild vegetables, and honey. There were also plenty of insects, such as grasshoppers and ants, to eat. I particularly loved the ants. I still know where to look to find fruits and berries, and I still know that there are bees you can follow to find their honey. And I still know that you should look down because there are mushrooms on the ground, but also snakes.

If I caught an animal I would take it to Taman's wife to cook. She cooked meat under a layer of ash, because ash is naturally salty. Sometimes she dried the little pieces of meat in buffalo dung, mixed them with bitter herbs and rice, and cooked them over the fire. The first time I returned to the village as an adult, almost twenty-five years later, I discovered that dish again and I ate so much I made myself sick.

The mountain land in the Mondulkiri region was ill suited for growing rice, so the entire village had to work together to grow our food. The forest had to be burned to create rice paddies. Every few years, the forest had to be burned so we could grow rice, and we would be forced to go farther and farther afield in search of good soil. The distances were vast, especially for my little legs, and sometimes we'd have to walk for several days. We had no carts or work animals like the Khmer had in their flooded rice paddies. Everything we brought back to the village we had to carry ourselves.

When the rice was harvested, several villages would gather around a fire to celebrate. We would sacrifice a buffalo to the spirits who lived in the forest and dance to the beat of the metal gongs. There'd be endless banqueting and lots of rice wine. I remember the earthenware jars being enormous, almost as tall as I was. We'd drink it straight from the jar, one by one, sipping through a bamboo straw. Even children were allowed to join in. I remember a great deal of kindness toward the children on these occasions. The Phnong people are good to children—not like the Khmer.

Our hills were so remote that probably no doctor or nurse had ever set foot in them. There were certainly no schools. I never saw a Buddhist or Christian preacher. And although my childhood coincided with the Khmer Rouge regime, I also have no recollection of ever seeing soldiers.

The Khmer Rouge had decreed that mountain people like the Phnong were "core people." We were examples for others to follow, because we had no contact with Western habits and lived collectively. Our forest and hills protected us from the suffering that engulfed the rest of Cambodia while I was a small child.

Pol Pot had abolished money throughout the entire country of Cambodia, along with school diplomas, motor vehicles, eyeglasses, books, and any other sign of modern life. But I don't think that's why we had no currency. The Phnong never needed money. If the grown-ups wanted something we couldn't make or grow or hunt, they traded for it. If we wanted a cabbage, we went to ask a neighbor who had planted some. He would give us cabbage without asking for anything in return. Now it's different: the people from Phnom Penh arrive on weekends or during the holidays in their big 4×4s with their pockets full of bills.

One day when I was about nine or ten, Taman called me into his hut and introduced me to a stranger. This man, like Taman, was a Cham Muslim. He was very tall and strongly built, with a thin nose like Taman and pale skin. I suppose he might have been about fifty-five, which is very old in Cambodia. Taman told me that this man was from the same place as my father. He used the word "grandfather" to refer to him, as all Cambodians do to show respect to the elderly. He told me that if I went with this grandfather, he would take me to my father's province and I would find my family.

Perhaps Taman really believed that this grandfather would take care of me. Perhaps he truly thought this old Cham man would help me find my father's relatives. Perhaps he was convinced that I would be better off living in the lowlands, with an adult to look after me. Or perhaps he sold me to this man, knowing full well that, at best, I would become his indentured servant.

I have tried many times to find Taman, to understand his reasoning, but I've since learned it's never possible to know what really motivates people.

At first I really liked this grandfather and was happy to leave with him. In my short life, not many people had offered to look after me. I thought this man was my real grandfather, someone who would adopt and love me. I thought he knew where my parents were. I put together a bundle with a tunic that Taman's wife had made for me, along with a wooden necklace and a short black and red cloth with green embroidery.

We began walking. We walked for a long time, along paths that took us farther and farther from the places I knew. He wasn't talkative, but neither was I. He spoke very little Phnong, and we were forced to communicate through rudimentary gestures.

We came to a place where people were swarming around a giant logging truck. It was the largest, most frightening thing I had ever seen. There was no way I was going to climb on the logs like everyone else—the truck terrified me. I had never even seen a bicycle before, let alone a motorized vehicle.

I backed away, but Grandfather glared at me and raised his hand menacingly. I didn't understand this gesture—I had never been hit—but I saw that his face had changed, that it was rough and angry, and it frightened me even more than the truck did. Then his hand struck me with a hard blow that knocked me to the ground. With my cheek bleeding, he pulled me up and onto the truck.

I knew then that I had made the wrong choice, that this bad man was not my grandfather and would never love me. But it was too late to go back.

2

The Village

When the logging truck dropped us off, we moved onto some kind of military truck that was carrying soldiers. After that, sometimes we rode in horse-drawn carts. There were people everywhere. A momentous change had dragged practically everyone in Cambodia back onto the road. A year or so earlier, in 1979, after four years of Khmer Rouge border attacks, the Communist government of Vietnam had invaded Cambodia. After the Vietnamese defeated the Khmer Rouge, they set up a new government, and starved, terrified people from every corner of the country began moving back to their home villages. When my journey took place, the country was still teeming with movement.

I knew none of this at the time, of course, but I was mesmerized by the crowds. The roads. The motorcycles. All the noise. The people looked beautiful, their skin so pale and their clothes exquisite. There were markets, with forks, bottles, string, shoes, matches, cigarettes, medicine, cosmetics, radios, and guns—all things I had never seen. There was so much metal, and so much color.

We were traveling southeast, across the border into Vietnam, though the concept of "Vietnam"—or even "Cambodia"—meant nothing at all to me then. Grandfather was delivering a load of sandalwood from the forest to a trader in Da Lat, in the high plains of southern Vietnam, and I helped him carry it. After Da Lat we traveled south, toward Saigon, and then began circling back.

One day I caught sight of a crowd of Vietnamese girls in their white tunics and trousers, like a huge flock of white birds. I was hypnotized. I suppose they were leaving school, but I had no idea what school was, nor any idea that I might go to one. I could see they were girls, but to me they looked more like angels.

Everywhere I went, I was horrified by the way people shouted at one another. In Vietnam, they were particularly scornful of me, a dirty, dark-skinned girl with no more brains than a lump of wood. They pushed me, yelled at me, insulted me.

I knew nothing and I asked nothing. I just kept silent. Everything was unfamiliar and dangerous. When Grandfather bought Vietnamese noodle soup, I tried to eat the long slippery stuff with my hands, though the soup was boiling hot.

As we made our way back north, toward the Mekong River, the flat countryside was unlike anything I had ever seen, flooded with rice paddies in every direction. To me it looked empty, as empty as I felt. I had a mission in this hostile flatland—to find my parents—but I was no longer sure that I would.

Eventually the road disappeared into the swelling waters of the Mekong River. The rainy season was coming. We got on a large, two-story ferryboat crammed with people and animals. We arrived in a Cambodian village on the riverbank. There were wooden houses on stilts, about forty of them, and red dirt paths snaking around the fields and into the forest. This was Thlok Chhrov, the "Deep Hole," so named because the banks of the Mekong are especially steep there.

Grandfather had a house in Thlok Chhrov, a little way from the river, made of woven palm leaves and palm trunks, with a bamboo floor. This village wasn't where he came from, and I don't know when or why he settled there. He had no wife or family. He spoke Cham, Khmer, Viet, and a form of Chinese, but nobody knew where he came from. Perhaps he too suffered during the terrible years of the Khmer Rouge regime.

Grandfather's house was small and ramshackle, half falling over, with one room, a sleeping pallet in the corner, and a charcoal brazier outside. It was my job to clean, cook, fetch water from the river, and wash the clothes. He beat some Cham words into me, enough so that I could understand his demands.

I was his domestic servant. Such things are common in Cambodia. It didn't matter if Grandfather had bought me from Taman or not. Now that I was there and he fed me and gave me lodging, I had to serve him. I owed him obedience.

Pretty quickly, I learned enough Khmer to understand the insults the villagers called out to me, the only Phnong in

the village. I was fatherless, black, and ugly. Like most
Khmer, the people in Thlok Chhrov see us Phnong as bar-
barians who are uncontrollably violent—some even say we are
cannibals. Of course, this is completely untrue. The Phnong
are honest people, true to their word and peaceful—unless, of
course, they are provoked by Khmer attacks. They also do not
beat and mistreat their children, which all the villagers in
Thlok Chhrov seemed to do. This shocked me.

The Khmer may scorn us as cannibals, but we Phnong
see them as treacherous serpents who never move straight
and will hurt you even if they have no need to eat.

Even though he was a Muslim, Grandfather gambled fre-
quently. He would take his small wooden chess set wrapped
in cloth wherever he went. He smoked cheroots of rolled-
up tobacco leaves and drank rice alcohol every night. When
he didn't have enough money for drink, his eyes would
grow hard. He would make me kneel and beat me with a
long, hard bamboo stick that cut into my flesh and made
me bleed with every blow.

I learned fear and obedience. Grandfather made me
work for other people to earn him money. Every morning
I had to fetch water from the river for several villagers. At
first, it was almost impossible to climb up the steep river-
banks with the heavy pails balanced on a stick across my
shoulders. I would slip and fall, the zinc buckets cutting
into the backs of my legs. Sometimes the cuts became so infected I could hardly walk.

In the evening, I had to use stones to grind rice into
flour before I could make it into noodles for dinner. That's

how it was in those days. If you had enough rice to eat, you were rich. We often didn't. When that happened, Grandfather and I would root through the food that the other villagers had thrown out for their pigs.

Grandfather often rented out my labor during the day. I worked in the rice paddies, near the river. In the dry season we rebuilt the small clay walls that kept the water in, and when the river began to rise, we planted seedlings.

Sometimes men and boys would appear from the forest and help us harvest the rice. They were Khmer Rouge fighters. In those days there were still large groups of soldiers in the countryside. There was a new, Vietnamese-backed government in power, but the Khmer Rouge didn't melt away into thin air. Instead, Pol Pot's army retreated into hiding.

For a long time, there were a lot of skirmishes in the countryside between the Vietnamese-backed government army and the Khmer Rouge fighters. In Thlok Chhrov we often heard outbursts of gunfire and exploding land mines and saw soldiers or Khmer Rouge fighters running through the village. When this happened, the villagers always ran indoors. They were terrified.

One time a boy who often worked in the fields with me—who wasn't right in the head—went looking for a buffalo at nightfall, even though there had been a lot of shooting. The next morning we found his body. His head had been cut off, and it had rolled into the scrub growth along the path.

I don't know which side was responsible—the Khmer Rouge or the Vietnamese-backed government—and I didn't really understand the difference. In those days, nobody talked in Cambodia. Nobody wanted to discuss the murder and starvation and death camps of the four years they had just lived through under the Khmer Rouge, or talk about how we were now living under Vietnamese occupation. They never talked about the Pol Pot time, the years of starvation and murder. It was as if they had blanked it out.

People learned from those years that they couldn't trust anyone—friends, neighbors, not even their own family. The more you let people know about yourself—the more you speak—the more you expose yourself to danger. It was important not to see, not to hear, not to know anything about what was happening. This is a very Cambodian attitude toward life.

I never saw parents explaining things to their children. They told them what work to do and they beat them. Many children were beaten every day, as I was, and some of them were much younger than I. It's mostly women, in these cases, who do the beating. Men hit more rarely, but when they do, it's more dangerous because they're so much stronger.

I dreamed of killing Grandfather, but it never occurred to me to slip away and try to make my way back home to the forest. That part of my life was gone forever—somehow it didn't seem possible for me to make my way back. I had discovered his true nature and I hated him. But I owed this man—even though he starved and hurt me, I belonged to him. He accused me of bringing him bad luck. Since I'd been with him, he said, everything was going wrong with his business, and it was my fault.

Sometimes Grandfather would leave on long trips, and

I would get relief. But most of the time he didn't work—he would sit at home, or gamble, and leave it to me to bring in the money. If I washed the dishes before I went to get fresh water, he beat me because there was no water to drink; if I went to get fresh water before I did the dishes, he beat me because the dishes weren't done. Sometimes I cried, but I grew accustomed to neutralizing my emotions. Who could I count on? People seemed to think it was normal that I should be beaten, since I was this small black savage, the lowest person in the village.

Most of the people I fetched water for never had a kind word for me. They were only angry when I came late, or if the water had spilled a little. But one elderly woman who lived alone was good to me. She used to fuss over my cut feet. One day she gave me a pair of blue rubber flip-flops— my first shoes. They rubbed uncomfortably between my toes, and they were very worn: the soles had two large holes and were so thin that thorns could pierce my feet through them. But they were shoes, and to me, that was really something.

From time to time I'd chat with her. I asked her why Cambodians were so horrible to the "black savages," why they accused us of being cannibals. While I was living in my village with those supposed savages, no one had ever beaten me, but in Thlok Chhrov, the villagers beat their children for the most trivial things. So who were the savages?

I remember the misery I felt during that first dry season in Thlok Chhrov. Huge mounds of rice stalks had been piled into haystacks, and I began to burrow holes into them, making nests in which I could hide from Grandfather. Sometimes I slept there. It was dark and hidden, and I felt safe.

After a few months I found another place where I could take refuge. A younger boy who worked with me in the rice fields used to go and eat at the schoolteacher's house, and he took me along too. Mam Khon, the village schoolteacher, was poor, but he and his wife looked after children. They had six children of their own, but they also fed a number of children who attended school but lived too far away to return to their homes every day. There were often twenty or more children in the house. It was a small house on stilts, made of plaited bamboo, with just one room. Everyone slept on the floor, and in the dry season the boys slept downstairs, on the bare earth, on beds laid out underneath the house.

Mam Khon's wife, Pen Navy, made cakes she used to sell, and sometimes she would give me one. I began helping her with the cooking and I would eat over there sometimes. She fed us all, though the family was so poor they often didn't even have rice, just rice soup.

Pen Navy was kind but stern, a rough authoritarian. She was half Chinese and had very pale skin. I thought she was beautiful. One afternoon while we were working she asked me why I didn't go to school.

The village school was an open-air classroom, with a thatched roof to give shelter from the rain. Mam Khon and another teacher had started it up again after the Khmer Rouge regime fell. There were crowds of laughing children, all in uniform—a dark blue skirt or pants and white shirt. Of course, I longed to go there, but I didn't think Grandfather would ever let me, and I told Pen Navy this. I called her "Aunty," as a sign of respect. For a while, we left it at that. It was clear to us both that Grandfather had the right to stop me from going to school if he wanted to.

Mam Khon himself hovered over the household like an apparition—he was a gentle, good man, but he rarely spoke. One day he found me crying, because the other children had insulted me. He bent down—he was a tall man, with a strong face and clear, dark eyes—and took my face in his hands. "You're not a savage," he said. "You're the daughter of my brother. My brother left to go to Mondulkiri with a woman and had a child there, and now I have found that child—it's you."

I had no idea whether or not I should believe him. But Mam Khon told me he would register me for school and said he would sort this out with Grandfather. Grandfather finally agreed that I could go to school as long as it didn't cost him anything. School itself was free in those days, because we were living under Communism, so he meant that I must still work for him and bring him money.

School was from 7:00 a.m. till 11:00 a.m. As long as I got up before dawn to fetch the water and bring home the money, I'd be able to wash and dress in time to leave. When I arrived, Mam Khon's colleague, Mr. Chai, a dark-skinned man, pinched and dry, said I couldn't register for first grade—I was already over ten and far too old.

Mam Khon told him a story to appease him. "She's my daughter," he said. "I lost her in the Troubles, but now I've found her. She's mine." This was how I got my name: Mam Somaly. Mam, like him. And Somaly, which he had chosen for me. I liked it.

I was so proud of my school uniform and was always careful to wash and care for it. The skirt and shirt were hand-me-downs, from Mam Khon's daughters, but they were beautiful to me. At last, I felt I was like everyone else. But the others didn't feel the same way. The village children called me *"khmao,"* which is like "nigger."

In Thlok Chhrov the darker you were, the dumber you were—this was an established fact. But I found it wasn't true. I studied and learned quickly. Soon I had learned mathematics and how to read and write Khmer.

There was no school in the afternoon, but we often had to do physical work there: every school was supposed to have a productive component, a vegetable garden or rice field. We planted jackfruit trees and coconut palms. I remember when we had to dig a huge pit in the schoolyard for a duck pond. It was hard, dirty work, but fun.

Sometimes in the afternoons we did military training in the neighboring field because there was still a war going on in the countryside. The soldiers taught us how to clean and handle rifles, how to shoot, and how to throw a hand grenade. We learned how to dig a deep pit with sharp spikes sticking up in the bottom of it—to capture men—and how to cover it with large dry leaves.

There were accidents. Sometimes during military training children were wounded. Once a hand grenade blew off a boy's foot. They took him away, but he died. This was sad but didn't seem to affect people a great deal. Death was random, normal—it was too routine to care much about one kid.

I remember the time the teacher asked us to list all the bad things that had happened to us under the Khmer Rouge. I had been living in the forest with the Phnong—nothing had happened to me under Pol Pot, so I gave back my paper blank. This teacher was Mam Khon's colleague, Mr. Chai. To punish me, he made me kneel for an hour in the sun on the thorny, hardened skins of dried jackfruit. My knees bled.

But other than that there were no real punishments in school. I was never tied down and lashed, as Grandfather used to do to me when he was drunk and out of money.

When we did military training I always took the role of the Khmer Rouge, because I wanted everyone to be frightened of me. I hated everyone—not just the children in my class, but all Khmer. But I didn't hate the Khmer Rouge fighters who sometimes emerged out of the forest to help us with the harvest, and I didn't hate the government soldiers who taught us, either. Occasionally the soldiers would give us things to eat—their rations allowed for milk and sugar. There were times I would have sold my soul for a glass of milk.

After about a year it got better. I had a new best friend, Pana, a boy who also worked in the fields and lived in a nearby village. We used to walk home together, though his walk was longer than mine. One day I had just arrived at Mam Khon's house when we heard a huge explosion from the direction Pana had taken. Mam Khon told me to take his bicycle, and I rode to Pana's house, still too small to reach the bike saddle. He had exploded. A rocket-propelled grenade had hit him. Apparently a soldier some distance away had thrown his RPG launcher on the ground and it had gone off. Pana's hand was in a tree, his arm was somewhere else—there was no body left, but I helped find all the pieces. Afterward I had nightmares about it. I went to the pagoda sometimes to pray for him. It was a long time before the nightmares went away.

Pana was my first friend and he was dead. I thought maybe I really did bring misfortune, just like Grandfather said.

In my second year in school, I came in at the top of the class. In those days, under Communism, the best students were given awards that were meaningful—bolts of cloth, milk, and rice. That year I received two bolts of cotton, blue and pink. I took them over to Mam Khon's house and his wife helped me cut out and sew a pink shirt with a heart-shaped pocket and a blue skirt. These were the first new clothes I had ever had, and they were my most precious possessions. I kept that blouse until I was in my twenties, when it burned with Mam Khon's house in a fire.

I began, shyly, to call Mam Khon "Father" a few months after he first took me to the school. It doesn't sound so unusual in Khmer. It's a term of closeness and respect, and other children called him "Pok" too. He was such a good man. He used to take me out fishing with him. He could never have survived on his minuscule schoolteacher salary, but he had a small, low rowboat we used to take up the Mekong in the evenings, trailing our nets along bamboo poles at different depths to catch various kinds of fish.

At around three in the morning we would tie up in midriver with other fishing boats—once you were away from the village, it was much too dangerous ever to sleep on the banks. Then, at dawn, we would make our way back and sell our fish on the shore. We gave the rest of the catch to his wife and daughters to ferment and make into *prahoc* sauce, or simply to dry. That way we could always trade dried fish for rice when the wet season came and fishing was difficult.

There wasn't much money in those days, and we traded for everything.

We never talked much—Father was a silent person. But we grew closer, spending time alone together on the river. He taught me how to mend nets and throw them flat and wide. I loved to be out on the Mekong, far from other people, even though I knew it wasn't particularly normal for a girl to be doing this work. Father's daughters never liked to fish. I suppose they thought it was disgusting, or maybe they were worried about keeping their pale skin out of the sun and the wind.

I tried to work hard for Father's family so they would let me stay there as much as possible. Father had six children, and the older ones were both girls. Sochenda was the eldest, about fourteen, and Phanna was two years older than I was, but I felt they were so far ahead—in school, in life, in everything. They were pale and beautiful, and they cooked and washed and studied during the day, in the house with their mother. They had time for study and were allowed to use an oil lamp to study by. This seemed miraculous—when I studied, it was by moonlight.

Sochenda and Phanna and the younger children were not overjoyed to have me as their new sister—at first I took to calling them Sister, and Pen Navy Mother. Still, they were not horrible about it. Even Phanna, the little princess of them all—the prettiest and the palest skinned—could be very nice.

Mam Khon's family was a traditional Cambodian family, by which I mean they never spoke about personal matters. It was not only inappropriate, it would give other people a hold on you. Children were taught that one should never give anything of oneself away, either in public or in private. Somebody who understands you can use your words to mock you or betray you. Confiding in someone means you are weak. Anything you say may one day be used against you. Better to hide what you think and feel.

There was a fortune-teller in the village, an old woman who lived near the riverbank in a hut even more derelict than Grandfather's. Everyone respected her and went to her for advice. I must have been about twelve years old when Pen Navy took us all there one day. I think she really meant to ask about her daughters' wedding prospects, which we all assumed were good—they were both so pretty and white—but the fortune-teller said Phanna would have an unlucky life with a lot of misfortune. Then she looked at me and said, "But the black one—she will have the three flags"—power, honor, and money. "She will travel in a plane and she will be a leader in the family. She will help you."

The other children hooted with laughter. Phanna laughed the loudest. "You'll have children so dark you won't be able to see them at night," she told me. It was good-humored, and I joined in the laughing. It just didn't seem possible that this would be my destiny.

Phanna didn't believe I was her sister in a real, biological sense or even her half-sister, and neither, to be honest, did I. I also wasn't sure about the story that these were my cousins. Another time when Father found me crying I asked him about it, and he told me he really was my father's older brother. He said his brother had left, and married a Phnong woman, and had a child, and that this man—his brother, my father—had a bad temper just like me. He held a mirror up and pointed to his eyes and mine, to his forehead and mine and said, "We are the same."

Another time he told me, "Your uncle, your father, it doesn't matter—the important thing is that we are together." I suspect he knows what really happened to my real parents, but he has never talked to me about it. Finally, I have listened to his advice: I no longer ask.

My breasts were growing, and Grandfather began touching them. He would roll heavily across the sleeping pallet at night and I would feel his hands on me. When he did this, I ran. I was fast—even today, people in the village remember me running. I would run down to the river in the dark and sleep there, on the banks where we kept the fishing boats. The reflection of the moon on the water calmed me, and I would curl into the roots of a tree or crawl into Father's boat and sleep on the nets. I continued to do my water duty and leave Grandfather the money that I'd earned, but I left as soon as possible in the morning, and during the day I tried always to be at school or at Father's house.

One evening a couple of months after we went to the fortune-teller, Grandfather asked me to get oil for the lamp from the Chinese merchant's where we bought our goods. The request sounded innocent enough—there was no electricity, so we used an oil lamp, and I often bought things from the Chinese merchant. He traded in rice and lent people money at high interest. He and his wife were respected in the village. Sometimes they gave me sweets or cakes.

But that day the merchant's wife wasn't there. The merchant had me follow him to the storeroom and offered me a cake. Then he threw me down on a pile of rice sacks and held me down. He hit me hard and then he raped me. I didn't know what he had done, but it felt as though he had cut me between my legs.

Then he threatened me: "If you tell anyone, I'll cut your throat. Your grandfather owes me a lot of money. If you talk to him about it, he will beat you. So shut it." He held out some striped candy.

I didn't take it. I refused and ran. I was bleeding, and I felt horrible shame, though I didn't understand what had happened. I went to the riverbank, and I told the tree about my pain and my disgust at these evil people, especially the Chinese man who had insulted and hurt me.

I tried to throw myself into the Mekong that night, at a place where the riverbank is very steep. I went under, but I couldn't help myself from swimming—it seemed that I couldn't make myself die. I washed up along the muddy bank a little farther down the river.

When I got back to Grandfather's, he beat me. He said it was because I was late. He didn't even ask what had happened to the oil I was supposed to bring. I realized somehow that he knew what had happened to me that night, and that he had sent me to the merchant on purpose.

I went back to the fortune-teller and I shouted at her. I told her she was talking nonsense, that she was an old madwoman who told lies.

Now I understand that Grandfather owed that Chinese merchant money and sold my virginity to pay his debt. In Cambodia, many men believe a virgin will keep you strong and imbue you with fresh strength—today it is widely be-

THE ROAD OF LOST INNOCENCE   25

lieved that raping a virgin will also cure you of AIDS. I can see now that what the Chinese man did to me was called rape, but at the time I had no words for it—I didn't know about penises. I thought he used a knife.

I also knew that I had to keep quiet, that this was something I could never talk about. Not only because of the fear the Chinese merchant had instilled in me, but also because it had something to do with things that were unspeakable in a Khmer family. Until today, I've never told my adoptive father about the rape. I felt good in that family, and I knew if I opened my mouth I'd be beaten, because Cambodian people don't talk about such things. It would only shame me and the people who heard me.

I learned to shut down all my feelings so that none of it mattered—so that it never even happened. Pain is temporary. It goes away if you let your brain go numb.

After that night, I no longer wanted to speak. I no longer wanted to understand Khmer. I closed myself up in silence and lived like a mute. The next time Grandfather asked me to go and get oil for the lamp, I refused, and he beat me. Then he went to get some of those red ants that sting so viciously it hurts for weeks. I don't want to remember that man.

After that night, I tried to avoid sleeping at Grandfather's house. But I always had to go back every morning and every evening to bring him money and cook his meal. Today, of course, I would leave. Today, I would probably kill him—but then, as a child, I just never thought of leaving. Maybe I was stupid, but there seemed to be nowhere I could go. I couldn't just settle in as part of Father's family—that would create conflict between my adoptive father and Grandfather, and Father hated conflict of any kind, with anyone.

So I continued to do chores for other families after school and take the money to Grandfather. One day when I was doing the dishes for an old woman, I got startled and dropped a glass, which broke. The old woman picked up a cane and started to beat me like a fury until my back was all bloody. At school I couldn't sit down, I was so cut up. I ran a high fever. My adoptive parents took care of me. They rubbed *moxa* on me—a traditional paste of herbs, which stings. It hurt so much I was crying. Father explained to me that in life one has to bear suffering. No matter how much it hurts, it is best to stay quiet.

He always used to say, "If you want to stay alive, grow a *dam kor* tree in front of your house." The *dam kor* is the silk-cotton tree, but the same word, *kor*, also means mute. To survive, you must be silent.

When the dry season came, Father began letting me and one of his young sons, Sothear, take out the fishing boat by ourselves. Sothear was about four or five years old, a quiet kid with hair that spiked right out of his head and huge, wide eyes. I was about twelve, but I liked having him around. Sometimes we went out in the evening and slept with the fishing families on the red earth down by the boats. Sothear helped me build a shelter of palm leaves and bamboo by the riverbank where I could sleep—it was just four bamboo poles and dried palm leaves for a roof. I made a floor out of dried rice stalks from the fields and I slept there.

It wasn't dangerous. A lot of people lived by the river. If I went out fishing at night, I would give a handful of rice to someone who was staying by the bank, and when I came back from the river my rice would be cooked, and we could share a fish. Every morning I would give my catch to Father and we would sell some, and if I had enough money to give to Grandfather, I could go to school that day.

In the wet season, when the Mekong swelled and flooded the banks, a lot of wood would come down the river. We would go out in boats to grab it and haul it in so we could dry it to burn in the fire. Sometimes we sold it, or traded it for rice, but mostly we kept it for Father's family.

At school, Mr. Chai began selecting children to train for a show of traditional Cambodian dance. Everyone was astonished when he picked me. He explained that at night, makeup would show up better on my skin than on the paler girls. Also, I had very long hair, unlike most of the other girls; under the Khmer Rouge, everyone's hair had to be short.

Mr. Chai trained us in the precise gestures of the Apsara, to curve our fingertips and hold our necks stiffly, like cranes. I didn't care much for the music or the dance, but people thought I was pretty, and I liked their surprised admiration.

We lived very collectively in those days. It wasn't like today, when individual families keep more to themselves, especially in cities. Cambodia was a Communist country. Every village was organized into groups called *krom samaki*— eight or ten families who would plant the rice together and share the labor of the village's few buffalo. After the harvest the group leader would ration it out; every family would receive perhaps fifty kilos of rice for the year.

I look back now at those days, and I think it was the best system for Cambodia. School was free, and it gave children a way out of poverty—not like today, when parents must pay huge sums of money for education and every diploma can be bought for a price. Hospitals were few and poorly equipped then, but they were practically free. Nowadays you could be dying, but if you can't pay they won't look after you.

Communism wasn't like life under the Khmer Rouge. People were no longer frightened. They no longer had to obey the orders of murderous young children who had been indoctrinated by the government. And so now they began to return to the old ways. The elderly ordered the young about instead of the other way round. Women no longer called their husbands "comrade," as they had to under the Khmer Rouge, but "older brother" or "uncle," and now they had to behave with the proper submission and respect.

Like all the girls at Father's house, I had to learn to chant the *chbap srey*, the code of good behavior for Cambodian maidens. It was part of the school curriculum—part of the government's desire to erase what the Khmer Rouge had done and go back to the old culture. All the girls in school had to learn to chant it, but Mam Khon wanted us to have it word perfect.

Ideally in Cambodia a woman walks so quietly you can't hear her footsteps. She smiles without showing her teeth and laughs softly. She never looks directly into the eyes of any man. A woman must not talk back to her husband. She must not turn her back to him in bed. She must bow before she touches his head, and if she walks over his legs she will become ill. In Cambodia, you must respect and care for your parents, and your husband is your master—second only to your father.

I was obedient, but I was not gentle. I seethed. I remember one afternoon when I was out fishing with Sothear. The two of us were on the riverbank when we caught sight of some rich people—people from Phnom Penh, the capital. To me they looked like gods, especially the woman—slender and pale, with clothes that looked new, and shoes with pointy toes. She talked softly and almost glided. She was so pretty, I was overcome with admiration.

I said to Sothear, "Maybe one day we'll be rich like them." He stood up and waved his arms, he was so excited. Sothear said, "We must really believe that—we *will* be rich like them. We must work hard at school and we can do it!" He told me he wanted to become a rich trader. I told him, "If I get married one day I want to marry a rich man too—a soldier, so he can kill my grandfather."

3

"This Is Your Husband"

Sochenda, Mam Khon's eldest daughter, was seventeen and due to pass her school-leaving certificate, a real achievement in our village. (I, aged fourteen, had still not quite finished primary school.) There was great excitement in the family; because if Sochenda passed she could go on to further studies, a rare thing for a village girl.

It was a national examination and it took place in Kampong Cham, the provincial capital, which was about three hours by bicycle from Thlok Chhrov. It was decided that we would all go there with Mother and spend the night at the house of one of Mother's aunts on the way.

That night, at this "grandmother's" house, Phanna woke me up to listen, because downstairs the old woman

and our mother were talking. They were saying how lucky
Mother had been to find a good man. We heard that when
she was young, our mother's stepmother had taken her to
another town and had sold her into a brothel. She had suffered a great deal. Father was a poor young man, but he
loved her. After he got his school diploma, he went to find
her in the brothel and he bought her freedom.

All this had happened long before the Khmer Rouge, in
the impenetrable time when Father and Mother were young.
I suppose it was probably the 1950s. Phanna and I were
overwhelmed by this revelation and we cried together. Our
mother had never told us anything about her past. She simply couldn't and she still can't. To this day we have never dis-
cussed it.

I think selling women into prostitution has always ex-
isted in Cambodia. People get into debt—it's easy, when the
interest is 10 percent or more a month. By working in a
brothel where the moneylender has an arrangement, a
daughter acts as collateral and repays the loan. Expenses,
such as food, clothes, medicine, and makeup, are extracted
from her account, of course, and the parents can incur
even more debts that will add to the money she must earn.

In other cases, the parents sell their daughters outright
to the brothel, essentially transferring their ownership of
her. A twelve-year-old girl might bring in fifty or a hundred U.S. dollars for her family, perhaps more if she has
canny parents and very pale skin. Other families just tell the
girls to do it, and they obey. The family goes to the brothel
every month or so to pick up her earnings. Daughters have
a duty to obey their parents and provide for them.

I know this is hard to imagine. But after all these years,

I can truly say that I think that for many parents, feelings have nothing to do with it. Their children are money on legs, an asset, a kind of domestic livestock.

About a month after we returned from that trip to Kampong Cham, Grandfather caught hold of my arm one morning when I was dropping off his money. He said, "Prepare your things and come to the house tonight." I did what he said—it never occurred to me to disobey him. That evening, when I went back to his house, there was a man there, and Grandfather told me, "This is your husband."

I didn't feel anything. I had made myself numb long before. Girls respected their elders, and I owed Grandfather obedience. This was just one more event in my life, after a lot of others. It's possible that I felt a little relieved: perhaps I would be leaving Grandfather's house. But I didn't want to leave with *this* man. I knew I was only exchanging one master for another.

We went to the temple—it was a wooden hut that the villagers had constructed in the grounds of the old Buddhist pagoda, which the Khmer Rouge had destroyed. A priest was there, but we had no ceremony to speak of. Usually there is a marriage ceremony and a big party, but Grandfather did not want to spend money on me. I wore my school skirt. We made offerings to the spirits at the temple, to respectfully request that they leave us alone; in Cambodia, you must constantly propitiate the spirits of the dead, or they will come into your house and cause you harm. The priest said, "You're married," and that was that.

My husband's name was Than, but I always called him "Pou," which means "uncle," as a mark of submission and deference. My new husband was older than I was. I was about fourteen and he must have been in his mid-twenties. He was a soldier. Tall, dark skinned, curly hair, white teeth. Quite nice looking and very violent. I hate to think about that man. Grandfather owed him money—he told me that later. The first night of my marriage I slept at Grandfather's house and my husband slept elsewhere. The next day we traveled, with Grandfather, to Chup, where my husband was stationed. It was about seventy-five miles away, and it took from dawn till late at night to get there—first on the boat to Kampong Cham and then on a truck.

Before we left, I went to Mam Khon's house. I told Mother that Grandfather had married me to a man. She told me, "Maybe it is for the best. You must leave with him, and perhaps it will be better with him than with your grandfather." She and Father must have suspected how often I was beaten, though we never talked about it.

My husband's house was a small shack built by the army amid the rubber plantations. It was one empty room, stained by red dirt and empty except for a cooking fire and a bamboo sleeping platform.

I hate marriage. It puts women in prison. On her wedding day the girl obeys her parents, and when the ceremony is over she is raped. What does a young girl in Cambodia know about sex? Nothing. I had already had sex, but I knew nothing about it. I didn't know what the Chinese merchant had put inside me—only that it hurt—and I had no idea that this was what happened in marriage.

I don't think I was unusual in my ignorance. One time, in school, when we were in military training, a boy stepped over a girl's back and she cried, because she thought she was pregnant. We were all like that. People told their daughters you got pregnant if you touched a boy's hand.

That first night my husband raped me on that platform several times, and when I resisted, he hit me. He grabbed my hair and smacked my head against the wall, then he slapped me so hard I fell down on the bed.

When it was morning I had to get up and make food. There was no explanation—no mercy or shame. We hardly ever spoke to each other.

I saw other people only when I walked into the village to buy food. I cooked grasshoppers, vegetables, dried fish, and he ate what I served him. If he didn't like it, he hit me.

That man—my husband—beat me often, sometimes with the butt of his rifle on my back and sometimes with his hands. With his fingernails, which he kept long and pointed, he gashed a deep scar into my cheek. He did it because I didn't smile, because I wasn't welcoming, because I was ugly, and because I was a death's head—that's what he called me.

He was very violent. Many soldiers are. When he was angry I would try to breathe as softly as possible, so as not to be noticed, because anything could set him off. To frighten me, sometimes he shot at me with his military rifle. At first it worked, but I grew used to it. Inside, I felt dead. When he raped me, I would try to disappear.

This was my life—another kind of domestic slavery. I never spoke to anyone about it. There were houses around us, with other soldiers and other soldiers' wives in them, but you don't talk about such things. Cambodians have a saying: You must not let the fire that is outside come inside your house, and the hearth fire must not be allowed outside. You don't talk about what happens in your household.

My husband was often gone, fighting the Khmer Rouge. The government couldn't afford to lose control of the rubber plantations, so the region was crawling with soldiers. When he left, I would quickly run out of money for food, with no idea of when he'd come back. Going back to Thlok Chhrov simply wasn't an option—Grandfather would only beat me, and I knew my husband would too, when he came back.

Chup was separated in two parts—the village itself, and then, near the rubber plantations where I lived, the clinic and the military grounds. The clinic was always full of wounded soldiers and village people who were brought there when land mines exploded as they worked in the fields, blowing off their legs or hands. There were land mines everywhere. The Khmer Rouge laid mines, and the government soldiers laid them to stop the Khmer Rouge from moving around the plantations—maybe there was even unexploded matériel from the American bombing of Cambodia at the end of the Vietnam War.

Nobody wanted to work at the clinic, especially at night, even though you were paid almost thirty pounds of rice every month. Nobody wanted to handle body parts and dead people. But all I wanted was work—I wasn't frightened of the dead. A dead body was like my body, no difference at all. Once or twice, though, I did step on a severed leg or arm in the dark—and I admit that was horrible.

Sometimes when land mine victims came in, all we

could do was amputate. If there was no anesthetic—and
there often wasn't—we tied the person down. There were
doctors at the clinic, but they weren't proper doctors—they
were just medics who had learned their job under the
Khmer Rouge. If they weren't there, we nurses had to carry
out the operations ourselves. Only one of us had any medical training at all: our chief nurse had done one course in
Phnom Penh for a few months.

We learned by trial and error—mainly error. When our
stocks of medication ran low, we diluted it. People died of
gangrene, of malaria, of blood loss. But the worst, to me,
were the women who died in childbirth. There I felt real
pity. One woman, who was expecting twins, suffered for
hours. We didn't know how to perform a cesarean. I was so
tired that after she died I fell asleep on the spot, on the
floor right next to her body.

When the young mothers had hemorrhaged on the inside, they would get ill and then develop a high fever. In the
West you call this puerperal fever. We interpret it differently. For us, it means a dead person has used the labor to
enter the body of the woman and perform a dance. A lot of
young mothers died of the fever. Those who survived childbirth went home to drink a glass of boy's urine, as custom
dictated. A coal fire was laid under their beds. They had to
eat a lot of pepper to get their energy back and to lighten
their skin. Highly peppered caramelized pork was served,
together with a few glasses of alcohol. We used traditional
recipes, but there was no real traditional medical expert
around.

Washing hands was not a habit at the clinic, and we often ran out of soap anyway. So many people perished in
pain. Obviously, all these years later, I can see that what we

did to the patients was awful. But we were poor and ignorant. It was a terrible situation and we did what we thought
best.

About six months after I was married, I got my period for
the first time. I was fifteen, and I thought perhaps a leech
from the lake had hurt me. I had no idea why I should
bleed, and I stayed home all day. My husband was away,
fighting. When I went back to work at the clinic, I asked my
colleague Pov, another nurse, about what happened. Then
the chief nurse arrived, and she was angry with me for missing work. She asked me for my excuse, and when I told her
my secret place was bleeding—that is what we say—she was
still angry, but she explained. She said this was what happened to women, and she took me to the cupboard where
she kept clean cloth, for bandages.

Pov hadn't had her period yet either. She was dark
skinned and her face wasn't pretty. None of the other
nurses liked her, but I did. She was about fifteen too. Pov
was an orphan, like me—she lived with her uncle, who beat
her. She told me he raped her too. Though I never told her
about my husband, that was when I realized that I wasn't
alone—that when my husband hurt me between my legs, this
happened to other women too.

There was no respite from men, even at the clinic. The
doctors there preyed on us, especially the pretty white-
skinned ones and the orphans, those who had nobody to
protect them. There was nothing we could do but submit.
At first I was spared, because I was ugly, and married. But it
didn't last forever.

The chief doctor came to find me one evening when I

was on night duty. He had already tried to sleep with me several times, but that night he used force. Afterward, he told me, "You're so ugly, you're lucky I'm doing this." The rape wasn't as bad as the words he said. Another doctor whom I liked and got on well with took advantage of the situation too. The choice was simple: let it happen or be fired and find myself with nothing to eat.

I felt like garbage, like I was nothing. I was also frightened of my husband finding out. In Cambodia a woman must not have sex with another man, and if it happens, many believe she should kill herself.

I tried. I swallowed a lot of Russian sleeping drops from the clinic. The next day I woke up stunned and bleary. When I went back to work a day later the chief nurse told me off.

Grandfather appeared again, from Thlok Chhrov. He needed money. And he had a letter for me—a letter! Phanna was to be married and she asked me to come, to be her bridesmaid. After Grandfather left, I got permission from the clinic to go. I paid a man to take me there on the back of his bicycle. I arrived the night before the wedding, and when I got to the house Phanna was getting ready.

I asked her, "Who is your husband?" She didn't know. She waved her hand at a clump of young men outside the house, watching the preparations. "Maybe one of them," she said. I asked her, "And are you glad?"

There was going to be a priest, several dresses to change into, makeup, cakes, a ceremony, but she looked at me emptily. I was fifteen, so Phanna must have been around seventeen by then. I thought she was very lucky to have been allowed to wait so long, though I knew some of the other villagers called my father's household the house of the old virgins.

Father was a teacher, an intellectual, and Mother was educated too. They had not forced Phanna to marry. Mother came and asked her, "Do you want to marry?" and Phanna answered, "As you wish," because that is what good girls do. That seemed normal to her, and it did to me as well.

She didn't ask me about sex, and I didn't tell her. Such things are never said. But I heard Mother say, "On the first night, you sleep facing your husband. If you turn your back on him that means you'll divorce. And you let him do what he wants." I realized that this always happened in marriage— that this was what marriage was about.

Grandfather wasn't in the village, and it was decided that I would stay at Father's house that night. Phanna had made me a dress. I was so proud at the wedding to be introduced as Phanna's sister; the husband's family just assumed that meant that this was my real father and mother, my real family. The husband was a boy of about eighteen, from a nearby village. He had been hiding in Thlok Chhrov from the government soldiers who had recently been coming around to conscript all the boys.

After the wedding, I returned to Chup. My husband returned, then shortly thereafter he left to fight again, this time much farther away. The fighting was becoming intense along the Cambodian border with Thailand. The Khmer Rouge forces were growing. They were now an organized army, based in Thailand. At the end of every year, the Vietnamese forces that occupied Cambodia would go on the offensive and destroy the guerrilla bases there, but after the dry season, as the rains resumed, the Khmer Rouge would

move back into the country. Now the government was
building a huge wall of land mines and mantraps along the
border, to stop the Khmer Rouge from coming across.

My husband left with his contingent for the border. The
weeks went by; he didn't come back.

A month or so after he left, Grandfather turned up
once more. The first time I gave him money, and he went
away. The second time I had no money to give him, and he
beat me. It had been a long time since he'd done that. Then
he told me, "Prepare your bag. We're going to visit an
aunty, in the city."

Aunty Nop

"The city" meant going to the capital of Cambodia. In those days Phnom Penh was nothing like the prosperous and wild city it is today. There was hardly any electricity. There were fewer vagrants in the streets. The buildings were wrecked and crumbling, the windows had no glass in them, and the roads were a jumble of stones, mud, and garbage. A decade after the Khmer Rouge had emptied the cities and sent all their inhabitants to work camps, the roads and basic utilities were still not repaired.

But I was bewildered by all the noise—by all the streets and the buildings. I had never been anywhere so wealthy and so crowded. The country was still Communist, but there were already nightclubs with local music, bars, and huge crowds of people.

There were giant, cacophonous markets selling everything from cooking pots to car parts, with massive displays
of food—fruit and vegetables that I couldn't even recognize,
and what seemed like acres of fish. There were crowds of
motorcycles too—more motorcycles than I had ever imag-
ined could exist—and black Russian bicycles, shiny and new.

Even girls rode bicycles here. Some people looked like
they were living in heaven. But I didn't think that Grandfather was taking me to the city for any good reason. I knew
nothing good could come from that man.

We arrived that first evening around dusk. Aunty Nop lived
in a small, dirty apartment in the narrow old streets around
the Central Market. We walked upstairs in the dark to the
second floor, because there was no electricity in the building. She eyed me sharply through the half-opened door.

Aunty Nop was about thirty-five, I suppose. She was a
Muslim Cham, like Grandfather, but she wore Western
clothes and had her hair styled in waves. She had a fat face
and wore too much makeup, with smears of paint and eye-
brows that she penciled high up on her forehead. I thought
she looked hideous, like a demon or some kind of evil
spirit. Her face was expressionless—I never saw her smile.

While she and Grandfather talked, I was told to wash. I
went into a pitch-dark bathroom. In the daylight that place
was filthy, and at night it was so small you felt it had become
your coffin. I had to wash myself there often; in that little
room.

That first night, Grandfather and Aunty Nop looked
at me and talked some more. They sent me to the bedroom, where there was another girl a little older than I

was—perhaps seventeen or eighteen. She had almond eyes, like a Chinese, but dark skin. She didn't say anything, and neither did I.

I saw Aunty Nop give Grandfather money. He turned to me and said, "Do what Aunty tells you. I'll be back." Then he left.

Aunty Nop lived with another woman her age and the woman's daughter, who was the girl on the bed. Her name was Mom. After Grandfather left, the women told me to sit still while Mom put makeup on me. Then they gave me a dress and shoes and said we were all going out.

When we left the apartment, it was already dark, and I stumbled over the debris in the street. They took me to a long, filthy, pitch-black corridor between two street-front shops. It led back into a dark courtyard and a warren of other alleyways. We went into a doorway and up a derelict flight of stairs. There were no railings left on the stairway— I suppose somebody had stolen them.

On the first floor, there was a kind of apartment. There weren't any walls or floors to divide this place from the stairwell—it was just a bare concrete floor, and you saw the beds and the blackened cooking fire as you walked up. There were many beds—rotting pallets made of woven grass. The place was filthy.

The woman in charge of this place was Aunty Peuve. She was a small woman, rather plump—plump for those days, anyway—with a mole on her lower lip and her hair in a bun.

I am writing about this place now because I never want to have to talk about it again. I never want to have to remember this again. It makes me vomit.

A man arrived, and I watched as he talked to Aunty Peuve. She signaled to Mom, and before she got up, Mom said, "You'd better know what this is. It's a brothel. Do what they say or they'll hit you." Then she left. Another man came in, and Aunty Peuve told him, "She is a new chicken, fresh from the country."

In the corner, nearest the wall, there was a bed walled off with a partition of sarongs. The man went in there. Aunty Peuve came to get me and when I said no, she hit me on the head. She said, "Yes or no, you will do it."

Her husband, Li, wasn't there at the time, but guards were there.

I went into the room, feeling frightened, as if I had been locked in a place with a hungry wild animal. The man was tall, he wore a shirt, he was in his thirties—maybe he was a policeman, or perhaps he worked in an office. He said, "Take off your clothes, don't fight me, I don't want to have to hurt you."

I was from the country—in Thlok Chhrov nobody ever took off all their clothes at once. We bathed wearing clothes and changed clothes under a sarong. I couldn't do a thing like that, not in front of a stranger. I fought him, and he raped me. But it wasn't easy, because I resisted.

So he did it again, to teach me another lesson. I was bleeding from the nose and mouth when he'd finished and felt dirty—blood and sperm were everywhere. It was morning, and when he left he said, "I'll see you tonight."

We went back to Aunty Nop's apartment, where I washed and slept. I felt a black, dark anger at Grandfather and at what he had done to me. In the evening it was time to put on makeup and leave again. When we got to Aunty Peuve's, she said, "Don't do that again. I gave you to that man because he is so kind, and I knew he wouldn't hurt you as some of the others would have done."

I remember that the next man was Aunty Peuve's husband, Li. He was fat and strong, and when I refused him, he hit me with his belt buckle. As a soldier, his foot had been blown off, so he walked with a crutch, and he had a beard. He smashed the crutch on me and raped me that night, and afterward so did his two guards. There was a Khmer guard with a puffy face like an alcoholic, and a hard-faced Chinese whose body was horrible, thin and coiled with muscles.

Cambodians are violent—they can beat you to death. Don't give any credence to those myths about the gentle Khmer smile. Men in Cambodia can seem gentle, but when they're angry they can kill you with their bare fists.

Afterward they took me down to the cellar. They kept animals there, snakes and scorpions. They weren't meant to kill us—they kept them to frighten us. It was a small room, totally dark, and it stank of sewage. They tied me up and before they left, they dumped the snakes on me.

That was the punishment room. I was often taken there, because I was difficult. The clients used to say I was ugly, or that I looked angrily at them—they often complained about me. The other girls said people had died there and they were terrified just to be taken down the stairs, because of the spirits. But I wasn't frightened of ghosts. The dead don't scare me. I cried, but it was because I had no parents, because I was helpless, because I had been raped and beaten, and because I was hungry and exhausted. I cried from emotion, not from pain. I cried from frustration, because I couldn't kill them. Grandfather, the guards—even my parents, who had left me to this. I missed having my real mother to love me and hated her for not being there. There was no love in my life.

I don't know when they let me out—a long time later—but I was there perhaps the entire next day. By the time Mom walked me out, my legs felt as though they weren't working properly. Aunty Nop was so angry with me she said, "I'm not feeding you," but I didn't want to eat anyway. It was Mom's mother who stopped Aunty Nop from beating me, because I'd had enough, she said. It was true, I could see double. She made me clean all day, and I wasn't allowed to sleep because I hadn't earned any money. Mom took pity on me and dabbed peroxide on my wounds. She knew what it was like.

After that I accepted the clients. There wasn't any choice.

During the day we lived at Aunty Nop's apartment. Later a third girl arrived. Aunty Nop specialized in new arrivals, girls straight from the countryside. She had the connections. But she rented rooms out to respectable people and she didn't want clients in her apartment, so at night Aunty Nop took us to Aunty Peuve's brothel.

It was Aunty Nop who owned us, but Aunty Peuve handled all the business. I suppose Aunty Nop gave her a cut. Aunty Nop and Aunty Peuve were *meebons,* women whose business is dealing in prostitutes. They looked after us, they fed us, they dressed us—though that was usually an expense we had to repay—and they lived with us. At night they rented us out.

Some prostitutes are sold to the *meebon* by their parents or relatives, or by their husbands. The price depends on their freshness and beauty, as well as the cleverness and connections of the seller. Today some girls are kidnapped into prostitution, but I don't think that used to happen so much when I was young. Most of the girls at Aunty Peuve's house were there as a kind of downpayment, to pay back a debt. They were supposed to work until they paid back the money their families owed—unless the families took out new debts that extended their daughters' servitude.

Nobody wants you back after you've worked in a brothel. The word for prostitute in Cambodia is *srey kouc*, "broken woman"—broken in a way that cannot be mended. You are forever ruined and your existence shames the family. Nobody wants people to know they have a prostitute in their family.

The clients were horrible. To them we were meat. They would say, "I paid a fortune, and you're not even pretty," and *smack*, hit you against the wall. Some of them liked hurting us and did it for sport. They were dirty. They stank. In my memory, their dirtiness is the most repugnant thing. That and the smell.

The soldiers and former soldiers were the most violent. They had a special kind of anger and ferocity. You felt it was uncontrollable, and they might kill you at any time. I remember one man who had been a soldier with Li and whose legs had both been blown off to two short stumps. He was sick in the head. I still have nightmares about him.

I tried never to look a client in the eye. I didn't pretend to like them. I closed my eyes and I often cried, though this never bothered anyone. Clients were policemen, shopkeepers, soldiers, construction workers. Young and old. Sometimes they were truck drivers or long-distance taxi drivers who rented beds on the sidewalks along the Central Market. They were just beds, wooden platforms with mosquito nets, which people brought out onto the sidewalks at night—you could rent one for about twenty-five U.S. cents. Being with a client on one of those beds was humiliating in another way.

It was common for a man, most often a Chinese man, to hire one of us and take us to a room where there were ten or twenty men. When the same people came back, we still had to go, even if we knew what was waiting for us. If we didn't go, we were punished.

We wore thick white makeup, like geishas—a kind of paste we made of white face powder from Thailand mixed into coconut oil. It made our skin whiter, which was what the clients wanted, and it hid the bruises.

The worst thing was how dirty I felt all the time. Aunty Peuve's brothel was filthy, the streets were filthy, the beds were filthy. I felt I stank of sperm. I hate that smell. Sometimes, even now, I'm invaded by the stench of it, usually after I've been talking to a girl about her experiences as a prostitute. Never during—she needs me to be controlled, to listen to her. But afterward, I'm overwhelmed, I feel sick, I feel I stink—it's as if I will never be clean. I keep a cupboard full of perfumed creams, but nothing takes the smell away.

I was always trying to get clean at the brothel. I'd learned in Chup to boil tamarind leaves in water, with salt, and wash wounds with it. I did that as often as I could. The other girls didn't seem to bother so much about cleanliness. We didn't talk much, either. When you're in a brothel, there's only one reality, which is the clients, and nobody wants to talk about that. And Aunty Nop and Aunty Peuve didn't like us talking among ourselves.

Grandfather came every so often to the apartment. Aunty Nop always gave him money. At first I said nothing to him—I was frightened, I think. But finally, I think the third time he came, I asked him why he had done this to me. He said it was none of my business. It was like I had no right to ask him—and I felt that, too. I had no right to ask him or to protest. I belonged to him, and this was just the way things were.

Occasionally Aunty Nop's husband would come to the apartment looking for money. He didn't like what she did to make it, but he didn't do anything to stop it, and he wasn't there much—he had another wife, and two children with her, and he too gambled a lot. Then he died. It was some kind of motorcycle accident, I think, about six months after I arrived in Phnom Penh. To pay his debts, Aunty Nop had to sell her apartment.

One afternoon she took us to Aunty Peuve's and left us there. Our ownership had been transferred. From now on we wouldn't just work out of Aunty Peuve's brothel, we would also sleep there, on the filthy pallets that were set up in two rows across the floor, in full view of the stairs. It was a horrible place, and my skin crawls when I think of it. Aunty Peuve slept in the corner. She had built a small room with cinder-block walls, which she kept locked, so I never went in there. The "room" where I was first raped was where Aunty Peuve's younger sister slept, on a big bed behind a wooden partition. We often slept there, all together, during the day. There was a bathroom behind a curtain where we washed with a scoop and a basin of dirty water.

I don't remember any windows. The buildings in the

alleyways behind the market were so crammed together, there wasn't much daylight to be had anyway. We lit the place with oil lamps and then, much later, when there was more electricity in town, a naked lightbulb.

We cooked over a brazier in the large room with the sleeping pallets. People going up and down in the stairwell used to stop and ask what was cooking. There were people who lived up there—I think they were *motodup* drivers, people you paid to ride you through the city or do errands on a motorcycle. I never went up to have a look.

During the day the guards slept in the room with us, and at night we worked. Aunty Peuve was not unpleasant to us, so long as we did as we were told and she talked to us sometimes. She was quite pretty, about thirty or forty I suppose, and had two small children who lived with us too. She didn't have such an easy life either. Li, her husband, beat her and he used to sleep with the rest of us constantly.

We caught diseases, of course, but we were lucky—there was no AIDS in those days. If I got sick I knew what to do, because I had worked as a nurse in Chup. I bought medicine, and I washed myself with tamarind—I think that probably protected me.

If a girl got pregnant she had to go to Aunty Peuve's friend who performed abortions. She would come back white and bleeding. But once the bleeding stopped there was no pity; it was right back to the clients, as soon as you could stand.

Sometimes clients came directly to Aunty Peuve's, and sometimes we stood out on the streets around the Central Market, just around the corner. Just like the villagers did in

Thlok Chhrov, most of the clients called me *"khmao."* I didn't fetch a high price, I was just a street whore. I didn't have regular customers like some of the other girls, perhaps because I didn't smile and I had dark skin.

But one time a man did seem to be interested in me. He came several times, and we almost became friends. He told me that he loved me and wanted to marry me. Part of me wanted to believe him—to believe that there was a way out.

I think Aunty Peuve might have caught wind of what was going on, because she told me she would have me beaten to death if I tried to get away before I had paid back the money she was owed. But the guards had grown used to us and they weren't as watchful. One night, when I was supposed to walk back from a client, I just didn't go back. I went to meet that man.

He was about thirty I suppose, ugly looking, but he could talk. And I wanted to believe him. The next morning he took me to the truck station. He said we should go to Poipet on the Thai border. He put me on the back of a truck that was heading for Battambang and he promised to join me there. There was another girl with me in the truck. When we got to Battambang that night, the driver and the other men on the truck raped us. My client had sold us to the truck driver.

I was sick. Sick of it all. Everything revolted me, and I vomited. The next day, when the truck stopped at Svay Sisophon, I jumped off. I remembered that my adoptive mother had some relatives there who came from China. I asked everyone I could and I finally managed to find them.

My cousin and his wife agreed to take me in. I minded their children and started to cook and do the washing for them. I thought I had found a place to stay. But after a week the wife left—she sold gold at the market, which took her away from home. When she'd been gone for a few days, my cousin threatened me with the acid he used to clean the gold. He raped me and he threatened to kill me if I said anything about it to his wife.

I decided that the whole world was the same, that all men resembled one another. After about a week of this I begged him to let me go, and he finally agreed. He even gave me a bit of money and a gold-plated necklace. When I asked him where to go, he said I should take a truck to Battambang and stay there overnight before getting a ride to Phnom Penh.

I had already made it to Battambang when I saw his wife looking for me. She grabbed my hair in the street and accused me of having stolen her necklace. She took me to the police station, where her husband confirmed her story. They threw me in the cells—I was clearly guilty, since the necklace was in my bag.

There were three or four policemen and they said, "If you want to get out you'll have to pay," but I had no money—they had taken it away. They took turns beating me and raping me all night. They said this was a way to pay, and they laughed about calling all their friends too. There was no point trying to resist. I only got hit harder, as if they expected it. In the morning they just let me go.

But I had nowhere to go. I couldn't go back to Thlok Chhrov. The only person waiting for me there was Grandfather. And for all I called him Father, Mam Khon had never suggested he could protect me from Grandfather. There was only the capital, Phnom Penh—that was all I knew.

I had no money and no necklace, but I convinced a taxi

driver to give me a lift to the city. I was only sixteen and I had MERCHANDISE written on my forehead. I know now how closely taxi drivers work with the brothels—they bring in the supply of girls, as well as the clients. I suppose that taxi driver must have recognized me or heard that I was missing—a dark girl with long hair, a Phnong savage with a scar on her face. He drove me straight to the Central Market in Phnom Penh. When he stopped the car, Li was waiting, with the guards.

It was as if there was nothing at all I could do right—no way I could escape. I felt I must somehow be carrying this destiny with me, as if the sign of some devil had fallen across my life.

Li beat me with his cane and tied me naked to a bed. Anyone who came was given the pleasure of looking at me. Despite everything I'd been through I was fundamentally modest, and this experience was horrible. That night his brother and all their friends took their turn with me while I was still tied up. It went on like that for a week. I was sick, shaking with fever.

I think that was when Li discovered something I was really afraid of. He was scientific about punishment: he wanted us completely cowed. He must have realized I wasn't terrorized by the basement room, because when I was taken down there I didn't scream helplessly like the other girls. I just glared at the guards and thought about how one day I would kill them. I always tried not to show pain, because I didn't want to give them the pleasure.

But one night Li dumped a bucket of live maggots on me. Hideous maggots, like the ones on meat. When he realized how much they frightened me, he began dumping them into my mouth and on my body while I was sleeping. I thought they would make their way inside me, into my body. That's what I have nightmares about, even now.

After Battambang, I said to myself that I had tried once to escape and I wouldn't try again. It would be the same no matter where I went. And for all her faults, Aunty Peuve was not horrible to us so long as we cooperated, though I know now that this is a slave mentality.

So I told the other girls, "It's worse outside. At least here we're protected from the police." And from that point on, I capitulated.

5

Aunty Peuve

I began doing most of the household work for Aunty Peuve. I needed to try to keep the place clean, and by doing all the cooking and cleaning and looking after the children, I bought myself some peace. Aunty Peuve understood that I had given in. She began to be much nicer to me, even friendly. She saw that I was clean and honest and she began leaving me alone in the house—she knew I didn't have to be guarded anymore. After a while she even began to let me go out to run errands. She knew I'd be back.

I can understand what I did then, I can understand what was done to me, but I don't understand what I felt—or why I did these things. I had just given up.

There were about a dozen girls living at Aunty Peuve's

house at any time. New girls would come in and have their
spirits broken, as mine had been. Rarely, a girl would leave
to live in a special, exclusive arrangement with a client.
More often a girl just didn't come back one night, and we'd
never learn why. Perhaps she escaped. Perhaps she was sold.

I know three girls who were killed. The first was a young
girl, Srey, who went out one night with a client and one of
the older girls, Chethavy. Chethavy was tall and pretty, and
she came from Kampong Cham. She had been a schoolteacher, but her husband and mother-in-law brought her
to the brothel.

Just before dawn one morning Chethavy came running
back to the brothel. She said that she had escaped, but the
client had shot Srey. Aunty Peuve didn't want any of us going out—she made us shut up and called the guards to deal
with it. But later that morning I went there to see. It was in
an alleyway like ours, just one street away, and when I went
up the stairs I saw the place—just a bare room, hardly big
enough for the bed, and not even a proper door, only a
curtain, to shield it from the stairwell. It was like a lot of
other rooms in Phnom Penh. Srey's body was gone, but
there was still blood on the floor.

The client was drunk and angry—we never learned any
more about it. Maybe Li made him pay something to com-
pensate for Srey's earnings.

The second girl was Sry Roat, a girl my age who arrived
about six months after me. She was very pretty, with white
skin, and men always picked her. I never learned who sold
her to Aunty Peuve: if a girl didn't talk, I didn't ask questions. I was walled into my own silence, dead to almost every
feeling, like all the girls. It was better to forget the past. You

had to endure every day as it came and hope only that it wouldn't be too violent. No other kind of hope seemed even a tiny bit realistic.

But Sry Roat desperately wanted out. And she thought that one of the men who used to ask for her a lot really liked her. She asked him to help her escape. She didn't know he was one of Li's friends.

When Li learned about Sry's plans he came upstairs and tied her up, right in front of us. We had been sleeping—it must have been about ten in the morning. He tied her arms and held a pistol to the side of her head and shot her brains out of her head. The other girls were crying, but I watched him. After he shot her, she fell over. Her head was hanging off the bed with the side of it half gone. He shot her again, two or three times, just for sport I think. Then he and the guards put her body in a rice sack and took it away.

Another time a girl was killed by a policeman who came in late one night. He wasn't a regular client, and it was very late, about 2:00 a.m. This girl—I can't even remember her name—didn't want to go with him. She was sick. He was drunk. The yelling woke us all—"Watch, all of you, because this will happen to you too one day if you don't obey"—and *bang*, she was dead.

Aunty Peuve didn't say anything. Everyone was frightened of that client because he was a policeman. Everyone in the neighborhood feared Li too, because he had a big stock of weapons and he was known to be very violent. But even Li didn't do anything about it. The policeman left and the guards took her away in a rice sack, just like Sry. We were garbage in life and garbage in death. They probably threw the sack on the public dump.

Most of the time I was silent. I did what I was told. I told my-self I was dead. I had no affection for anyone—not for Aunty Peuve's children, nor for any of the other girls. I did have some pity. If another girl had had a really brutal time or if she was badly hurt, sometimes I would volunteer to go to a client in her place. But mostly I felt nothing but hatred.

One time, though, I let two girls escape. They were new, straight from the countryside, and they looked alike, with long, dark hair. Aunty Peuve had them tied up, and they were crying. I knew what was waiting for them—the life that would be taken out of them. They would die internally, like me. And for some reason I didn't want that to happen to them too.

They weren't the first new girls I'd seen, or even the youngest—they were about fourteen. But when Aunty Peuve left them with me to go out, I untied them. I just said, "Don't stay here." I had nothing else to say—I really didn't talk, and there wasn't anything else I needed to say. They looked at me—without a word—and they ran.

I was punished. Li hit me hard—his children were cry-ing, because they liked me a lot. By then Li had electrodes hooked up to a kind of car battery. They burned your skin. I still have the marks. I was taken downstairs and beaten for days, three or four, I think. I felt like I was bleeding inside. Afterward I couldn't work for a few days and when I started working again I had to work even more to reimburse the losses—the girls cost two gold *chi*, about eighty U.S. dollars. After that, I calmed right down and never did anything like it again.

My punishment was harsh, but the way they punish prostitutes today is far worse than anything I ever had to suffer.
When I was with Aunty Peuve, except for that one time with
the electricity, the punishments were mainly beatings and our
own fear—things like the snakes. Now I see girls in brothels
with nails hammered into their skulls. That sounds unbelievable, but we have photos. Girls are chained, beaten with electric cables. They go mad. We've rescued several children from
brothels who have completely lost their minds.

Recently some dead girls were found in the sewer near a
brothel: they had drowned. Another time, after a fire, the
police found several girls' bodies, still chained up. They
know who owned that brothel—everybody does, but he isn't
picked up and nothing is done about it. He has too many
connections, and the girls are nobodies.

The cuts and welts we see on escaped prostitutes these
days are unbelievable. The clients do it, or the pimps.
Maybe it's the influence of Chinese films, which are full of
torture scenes. The pimps watch them avidly, like a lot of
other men.

Nowadays the girls are much younger too. This is because men in Cambodia will pay a thousand dollars to rape
a virgin for a week—it's always a week, for a virgin. Sex with
a virgin is supposed to give strength, to lengthen a man's
life span and even lighten his skin.

To make it clear they offer true, bona fide virgins, the
brothels today sell children. Often they are very young
girls, just five or six years old. After the week is over, they
sew the girl inside—without an anesthetic—and quickly sell

her again. A virgin is supposed to scream and bleed, and this way the girl will scream and bleed, again and again. They do it maybe three or four times.

Brothels that specialize in virgins for rich men are evil places. After a few months the girl drops in price and they sell her on. There's a big call for novelty, and most of the brothel keepers have family connections—there's always a cousin in the trade, in Battambang or Poipet, who will take a girl or make a swap.

People believe sex with a virgin will protect you from illness, which is another reason for the high price of a young girl. People use them like a medicine, to cure AIDS. But the little girls tear much more than grown women, and they get AIDS more easily.

When I lived at Aunty Peuve's there was no resewing and no small children. Aunty Peuve dealt in young girls, but they were never much younger than twelve. When a girl came in from the countryside, she just told the clients, "She's a new chicken," but I don't know if that meant she got more money. I think in those days there wasn't the same market in virginity as there is now. Under Communism, there was a lot less money.

This was ordinary prostitution. Stinking mouths and bodies, dirty rooms, violence. The blows hurt, but the act itself was much worse. Sometimes there would be only two or three men a day, sometimes many more. If there weren't enough, Li would tell Aunty Peuve not to feed us, so we'd try harder. If there were too many, you hurt inside and out, until you managed to shut all feeling off.

It's still happening, today, tonight. Imagine how many girls have been raped and hit since you started to read this book. My story doesn't matter, except that it stands for their story too, and their stories are why I don't sleep at night. They haunt me.

Mom, the dark-skinned girl from Aunty Nop's house, used to go and see her mother often. She had a different kind of arrangement with Aunty Peuve, semi-voluntary. Aunty Peuve paid Mom money, and Mom used to take it over to her mother every week. Sometimes I went with her: I had nobody else to visit in Phnom Penh.

Mom's mother accused Mom of being lazy and she used to beat her a lot—there was never enough money to make her happy. She still rented a room from Aunty Nop, just a few streets away from where we'd all lived. Sometimes Aunty Nop would be in when we visited and she'd give me tea or something to drink. I hated her—I never liked that woman—and I didn't like being there, but she pretended to like me. So I sat and answered her if she asked me something.

It must have been sometime in 1987 when Aunty Nop told me that Grandfather was sick. Apparently he had been coming to see her regularly, to get more money. I suppose he was extending my stay with Aunty Peuve, though in those days I had no idea what the system was—I didn't know I was working off an ever-swelling loan. Now, Aunty Nop said, Grandfather was ill and he was asking for me.

I didn't go back to Thlok Chhrov to see him. I was seventeen years old by now and I had been a prostitute for almost two years. I had watched Li shoot my friend Sry Roat. I was full of anger and I wasn't afraid of Grandfather anymore. I also had no desire to return to the village. If people had been nasty to me before, when I was just a child, they would be truly evil to me now that I was a prostitute.

Aunty Nop didn't make any comment when I told her I would stay in Phnom Penh instead of visiting Grandfather. She neither approved nor disapproved—she had done her duty. Several months later, when she told me Grandfather was dead, it was the first time in years I felt happy. I had often dreamed of killing him.

But his death didn't mean I was free. Aunty Nop said I must now repay all of Grandfather's debts. After he died, all kinds of people claimed he owed them money, and I had to pay them. I don't know how to explain this, but that was just the way it was. He had looked after me, I was his "grandchild," and I was his indentured servant, so his debts became mine.

I didn't try to protest. I just lived from one day to the next. I had never received money from any client—they just paid Aunty Peuve—so it made no difference to my life. My body was nothing, of no value.

By now I understood that I was actually paying back a fixed sum of money and that one day that sum would be paid. I don't know if it was Mom who explained it to me or whether it was Aunty Peuve who showed me the account. She trusted me now; she talked to me and dealt with me more like an equal. I was eighteen by now and more of an adult.

Aunty Peuve's business wasn't doing very well—she was down to about four girls. Li used to gamble a lot, and maybe that was why things were going downhill. I had also been sick for a while with a high fever. This meant that I was just a cost to her—my food can't have been very expensive, but there were fewer clients, and I wasn't earning much.

I had been working for Aunty Peuve for three years

when she let me know I could go. It was about eight months after I heard that Grandfather had died. She didn't say it outright—she told me one of the clients had offered to marry me and advised me to accept.

This man drove a *motodup,* a motorcycle taxi, and he was a really nasty piece of work, and dirty too. There was something about him that I'd always disliked and I always tried to avoid going with him. He was a regular client of one of the older girls, Heung. After being with him, Heung always came back bruised and hit—though that wasn't unusual.

Perhaps it was out of kindness that Aunty Peuve suggested I marry this man, because I'm sure that by then I had paid back Grandfather's debt many times over. But I have to doubt it was a pure expression of friendship. Maybe I was becoming less profitable to her. Actually, I wondered whether the *motodup* driver had offered to purchase me and Aunty Peuve was trying to trick me into leaving.

I turned down the offer. I didn't think I would be safer or better off with the *motodup* driver—he wasn't even rich. I knew by then that on the streets of Phnom Penh a girl is a commercial product. Even if I left Aunty Peuve, if I were poor someone would just sell me again. And that would be okay because it would make him rich.

I told Aunty Peuve I would stay. But this experience made me realize that there might be some way out of the brothel for me. There was nothing else I knew how to do, and nowhere else that I could go except another brothel, but I began to suspect there was a way to get out, like Mom had done, and I longed for it.

About a month after the *motodup* driver offered to buy me, another man came along. His name was Min. He was an itinerant businessman, involved in different kinds of trade—an ordinary client, though he wasn't as brutal as most of them.

I felt nothing at all for Min: I saw only a staircase I could climb, a way out. When he asked me to come and stay at his place, I started spending nights there. His shack was on the roof of a building near the riverfront, in a neighborhood we call "Four Rivers," where the Tonle Sap meets the Mekong. It was like a shed, made of random pieces of wood and metal sheeting, like a lot of other shacks all over the city. Min fed me and looked after me for two days, and then he told me he had no money left and I would have to go out and earn some for us both. He said he was starting a business, a shop we could both work in—he was vague about it, and I didn't think it was true.

We didn't have a formal arrangement. I hadn't officially left Aunty Peuve, but I began to work for Min. He used to watch out for me on his motorbike while I waited for a client to come by. I worked for Aunty Peuve too. For a couple of weeks I worked out of Aunty Peuve's apartment most evenings and for Min during the day, to make money "for us both." Then I realized that he was lying to me just like everyone else and I stopped.

Eventually I went back to Aunty Peuve's place. Min was really angry about it. Months later, he was still hassling me for money. And I became even more convinced that there was only one way I could get out of prostitution. I would have to find a man who was rich.

6

Foreigners

Sometimes—very occasionally—I would go into a rage. Maybe it was the Phnong in me: I would suddenly crack and rebel. The first time was when I let the two girls go and got so badly punished. The next time it happened was at the end of my years with Aunty Peuve. I shot a client.

It might have been New Year's Day in 1989, because the white people were all celebrating something. There were suddenly a lot more white people around in 1988 and 1989, and they weren't Russians and East Germans, as they'd always been. They were French and Italian and English people, and they had come to Cambodia because the Vietnamese soldiers were leaving. There were peace talks taking place in Paris, and the new white people were mostly humanitarian workers from organizations like the Red

Cross. Anyway, on that night when I shot the man there was a lot of shouting and laughing from drunken white people in the street—it was some kind of special day.

The client who had hired us was a man who always used to pick Mom and me. We would try to slip away from him when he came to Aunty Peuve's but it was always us he chose, though sometimes he chose other girls to come along too. He would always take us to a room where there were ten or fifteen men and they were always drunk. One time they drugged us. They gave us something to drink, and when we woke up we were covered in bruises. This man was always complaining about us to Li, so we'd be beaten. He was a big man, a brute who liked to use his fists.

Mom was back at Aunty Peuve's by that time, because her soldier friend, Roen, was away, and her mother had run out of money. That night, the client chose just the two of us. He drove us all the way to Ken Svay, a village outside Phnom Penh—maybe it was where he was from. He was drunk and it was late, and there didn't seem to be any other men with him. He took us to a room above a bar and he kept drinking.

It was very late and he'd been drinking steadily for hours when he began to yell at us and shoot at Mom. He wasn't shooting wildly—he was sitting at the table with a gun and shooting around her, just to scare her, like my husband used to do to me when I lived with him in Chup. He was angry, but he was enjoying it. Then he went to the toilet—he was so drunk he left his gun on the table. I picked it up.

Mom said, "Do you know how to shoot?" and I looked at her and went into the bathroom. The client was frightened—he said, "Don't do that, *khmao*"—and I shot at him. I was just so angry.

The bullet hit his leg. He was yelling but probably nobody could hear him, because of the noise in the street. I really wanted to kill him, but I thought about his wife—of course this man had a wife, and probably daughters too. So we tied his mouth up with his scarf and left him there and ran. He was really scared, and so were we. We ran as far as we could, and at dawn we found a *motodup* to take us back to the brothel.

That man did come back to Aunty Peuve's to complain eventually, but it wasn't for weeks—I think he was too frightened to do it before or maybe he was in the hospital. By that time I was already protected; I had found Dietrich.

Dietrich was a humanitarian worker with one of the big relief agencies in Phnom Penh, and one night he picked me up on the street. I saw the Toyota Land Cruiser with the humanitarian agency's logo on it drive slowly past me as I stood on the sidewalk, and then it circled around the block and came back and stopped.

Aunty Peuve was watching, as usual, and she handled the negotiations and took the money. It was the first time I had ever had a white client, and I thought he looked strange. He was about twenty-eight, much taller than any Khmer, and his hair was a long stripe down the middle of his head and short everywhere else.

Dietrich didn't just take me to a room of some kind, either. He took me to a street stall first, because he was hungry and wanted to eat. He didn't speak more than eight words of Khmer, and I certainly spoke no Swiss German, but he bought me dinner, which no client had ever done, and he tried to talk to me. He clowned around, mimicking things, and he tried to make me laugh. He pushed at the corners of my mouth so I would smile. When he took me to the guesthouse room he'd rented, it was the first time I'd ever seen a mattress. I was very unsure of myself. I didn't know what this foreigner was going to do to me. I thought maybe white people were different from Khmer. He sat down on the bed and patted it, for me to sit beside him, but when I sat down it felt soft—as if something were swallowing me—and I leaped up, frightened. This client laughed again and motioned for me to go in the bathroom and wash myself.

I was glad to have a reprieve from the mattress, which was genuinely scary, but the bathroom was strange too. It was very clean, but I had to look everywhere for the basin of water to wash myself. The only water I could see amid the shiny taps and empty white containers was a tiny amount at the bottom of the toilet. I had never seen a toilet like that, so I thought it must be the washing bowl. I splashed the water on my face, thinking, That's all the white people use to wash in?

When I went back into the room, Dietrich said to me with gestures, "Did you shower?" and I shook my head. He came back into the bathroom and turned on a shiny thing, like a snake, and it flashed to life, spitting at me. I jumped back, certain that thing was evil and would hurt me. I was frightened, thinking it might be a phantom of some kind, and I ran out screaming. Dietrich had to explain running water to me—the pipes, and the showerhead. It was another world. I was scared that the water would flood everything and I would drown. Despite my fear, I tried to have a shower, all wrapped up in a towel and leaving the door open so that I could run out if the phantom came back. That was the first time I ever used proper soap, and I remember how good it smelled, like a flower. Soap is expensive, and the only thing we ever used was soapflakes, the kind you wash clothes with.

After my shower Dietrich did pretty much what all the clients did, although he didn't hit me. He also drove me back to Aunty Peuve's place and gave me extra money, which no client had ever done before. It was a lot. He paid fifty U.S. cents to Aunty Peuve for me, but he gave me twenty dollars.

Dietrich used to come looking for me at Aunty Peuve's brothel, but I could tell he didn't like doing that. Sometimes he'd send his translator for me—a Cambodian man who worked in the office of Dietrich's relief agency. When I was with Dietrich, I would spend all night with him in a nice room in a small hotel or at one of his friends' apartments. In the morning, he would always drive me back, with money for Aunty Peuve and money for me.

Sometimes Dietrich gave me enough money so that I didn't have to work for Aunty Peuve at all for a few weeks. I'd give most of it to her and then leave and spend a couple of nights with other girls I knew. One of them was Heung, who was living on her own now. Aunty Peuve had thrown her out—she was at least twenty-eight, which is old for a prostitute, and she was sick, so she wasn't earning much money. But Heung was still selling herself on the street, though she didn't have many clients. She could barely pay for the shack she rented from another woman, Phaly, who was also a prostitute. Their shack was on a rooftop, and it was falling apart, barely even a shelter.

I used to bring Heung presents and stay with her for a few nights. Or I'd visit Chettra, a girl who had left Aunty Peuve to be the live-in mistress of a Khmer shopkeeper. Chettra was from an ethnic minority, like me. She was Stieng, from the hills about eighty miles south of the village where I grew up. She and I liked to eat the same food, and I loved to go to her place, when her shopkeeper was out, to cook spicy chili dishes.

After a few weeks had gone by, Dietrich stopped renting hotel rooms and started taking me back to his house. He lived in a big villa near the Calmette Hospital, with a gate and a guard to open it. There was a porch with French columns and silk cushions on the sofa and a cleaning woman. When I first saw it I could not believe it. I was used to clients who took me to moldly rope beds on the street.

I didn't "love" Dietrich. He was nice, though. He was kind, he didn't hit me, and he did his best to communicate, although he never learned much Khmer. We spoke in gestures. I was nineteen years old and I learned a lot from him. The first time Dietrich took me to a restaurant for white people, I made a fool of myself. It was at the Thailan Pailin, a really nice hotel now. I could smell chicken—it smelled unbelievably good. I had a pretty, shiny pink dress on—I had recently had it made, but I could tell my date didn't like it.

And when I asked for chicken, it came roasted—a whole thigh in one huge piece, with a knife and fork on either side. How would I know how to eat with a knife and fork? In Cambodia, we cut meat into tiny pieces and we eat with a spoon or with our fingers. I knew that if I ate Cambodian style here, people would take me for a savage.

So I bravely wielded my utensils, but at each attempt to cut the chicken, it wandered off to one side of the plate or another. The more I tried, the more difficult it became. While I waited to capture it, I swallowed my rice. I couldn't ask Dietrich to help, because we could hardly speak to each other and he seemed to notice nothing. My frustration grew from one minute to the next. Dietrich made a sign asking me, "Aren't you going to eat your chicken?" I shook my head. Time passed and at last the waiter took away the dish, which was literally making me salivate. That night, I dreamed of the poor chicken I hadn't managed to eat.

One night when I was with Dietrich in his Land Cruiser, I caught sight of my adoptive father, the schoolteacher, and one of his young sons. They were riding on a motorbike beside Dietrich's car and gesturing to me. Father looked wrinkled, exhausted, and really poor. I asked Dietrich to stop the car and I got out. Father told me he'd been look- ing for me—he had heard I was in a brothel. He said he had sold his fishing nets and his boat so he could come to Phnom Penh and search for me. He wanted to take me back to the village with him, where I'd be safe.

I was flooded with shame. I was dressed indecently, in a foreigner's car—I looked like a whore and I was one. I couldn't go back to Thlok Chhrov with this good man, whom I had shamed, and face the villagers there as a Phnom Penh prostitute. I couldn't do it, and I couldn't face Father. I got back in the car as fast as I could and told Dietrich to drive away. I was so ashamed, I didn't even think to give my adoptive father any money—I didn't even say a word to him. As we drove off I was crying.

Dietrich gave me money, and I enjoyed the freedom it gave me and the clothes I bought with it. They were just trousers and T-shirts, but they were clothes that didn't say "whore"— the kinds of clothes a nice person might wear. Still, Dietrich was just another client, and I couldn't count on him. He never said when we might see each other again, and he was often away for weeks at a time working for his humanitarian agency. When I had to, I still worked for Aunty Peuve.

But now, instead of standing by the side of the road around the Central Market, I went out to a hotel called the Samaki, which today is called Hotel Le Royal—Cambodia's most luxurious establishment. There were many foreign men there, and I began waiting for them at the bar. Cambodians thought my dark skin was ugly, but foreigners seemed to like the color, and my hair, which fell all the way down my back. Foreign men didn't seem to beat girls as much as Khmer clients did. They took you to nicer places. And they paid more.

Dietrich suggested I become his "special friend." (He had to explain this through the translator, so I would really understand.) Under this arrangement I would live with him, and he would give me spending money. He handed me a key to his house. I didn't even go back to Aunty Peuve's place to pick up my things.

I liked the luxury and the comfort of living at Dietrich's house. It never felt like I really lived there, though. I never learned how to cook properly in his kitchen, which always frightened me, and he always ate out anyway—often with his friend Guillaume, and always European food, in restaurants for foreigners, never rice and *prahoc* sauce and spices.

Still, Dietrich was a good man. He didn't like that I cried when we had sex, but we mostly did it in the dark, so he didn't always notice. He was also rich—for Cambodia, anyway—and he was white, which meant he had power, and because of this, nobody could bother me anymore. When Min, the man I'd lived with briefly in the rooftop shack, tracked me down and yelled at me for money, the guard at Dietrich's gate sent him away. That felt good.

But Dietrich's contract in Cambodia was drawing to a close, and he had to go back to Switzerland. About six months after I first met him, he brought his translator to the house to talk to me because he wanted to be sure I would understand. He said he was leaving forever, but that he would be glad to take me with him if I wanted to go to Switzerland.

It didn't seem real to me. I knew nothing about Switzerland and nothing, really, about Dietrich, though I'd lived with him for several months. My friends, Chettra and Mom, thought that perhaps he planned to sell me once we got to Europe. I too distrusted Dietrich in a way—I couldn't understand him, could never figure out why he did things. I thought that if I left Cambodia for a place where I would understand nothing, not even the language, I might find myself a lot worse off.

Before he left, Dietrich gave me a thousand dollars. (In Cambodia we use U.S. dollars for large sums; the national currency, the riel, is only for small sums of money.) It was an unimaginable amount of money to me, something like a hundred thousand dollars today. He had his translator tell me that with this money he wanted me to buy a motorbike, go to school, and maybe start up a business—he said that I should use it to make a new life for myself. Dietrich didn't want me to have to go back into prostitution. He was a decent man.

After he left I went back to Aunty Peuve's and I gave her
a hundred dollars. I don't know why I did that, but it's what
I did. I suppose that, like an idiot, I thought she had feelings for me. I also gave a hundred dollars each to Mom and
Chettra. I couldn't find Heung—she had left her shack, and
nobody knew where she'd gone. But I gave all the girls at
Aunty Peuve's house fifty dollars each. I bought them their
freedom, if they wanted to take it, and that is something I've
never regretted.

I think that was the last time I went to Aunty Peuve's
brothel. I have avoided that street ever since. When I go
near it my skin crawls and I begin sweating. I don't have the
strength—I always take another route.

Now I had to figure out what to do next. Before leaving,
Dietrich asked his friend Guillaume to look after me. Guillaume was Swiss too, and I owe him as much gratitude as I
owe anyone in this world. He let me stay at his villa and he
found me work, cleaning house for his friend Liana, who
was Italian. I earned twenty dollars a month. It was enough.

Guillaume took me to the Alliance Française building
downtown and had me sign up for French lessons. I didn't
have enough money left to pay, so Guillaume paid for it
himself. He never tried to touch me, never took any advantage; he was only being kind to another person. He is still
my good friend.

I liked going to the Alliance Française. There was no
uniform, of course, but I bought a dark blue skirt and a
white shirt and ironed them carefully before every lesson.
They meant something to me, something clean and honest,
like a mask over the filth that was underneath. I had a deep

desire to pretend to be a nice young student at the Alliance Française, with books under my arm.

I didn't learn much—French was hard. When Grandfather sold me to my husband in Chup, I was just finishing primary school. I could read and write curly Khmer letters, but the straight letters of the Roman alphabet were very different. It was just one class a week, but little by little I began to understand some words. I loved trying to learn something—and I worked hard at it.

Sometimes I used to go out with Chettra and Mom to the nightclubs that Dietrich had taken me to, where there were a lot of foreign men. Mom was working for Aunty Peuve again, and when we went dancing she would pick up clients. I met some men too. Hendrik, an American who worked in Singapore. Dino, an Italian. It wasn't like prostitution, because these were longer relationships than just one night, but it felt close to it.

I had been a prostitute in Phnom Penh for four years, and I didn't know how to get out of the whole system. I wanted to, but in my mind I was trapped. I wasn't worth anything. I was *srey kouc*, broken and unmendable. I was dirty and I could never hope to become clean again.

Guillaume knew a lot of people and he had parties. All his friends claimed to fall in love with me, which meant, of course, that they wanted to have sex. These were rich white people who worked for embassies and cultural centers and big businesses. They came to Cambodia for a year or two and rarely spoke much Khmer, just like they didn't eat local food.

But one night I met Pierre. It must have been in 1991.

He was tall and nice looking in a raggedy kind of way. He was French, about twenty-five, and he worked for a French humanitarian agency doing lab analysis. I was twenty-one and I had never met a foreigner who spoke such perfect Khmer.

Pierre asked me questions about myself. Dietrich had tried to make me laugh and then had sex with me, but Pierre asked me a thousand questions. He asked where I came from, how I had come to be a prostitute, why I was doing it, and whether I wanted to get out. He listened. And I, who had always been silent, began to find that I was talking.

We talked from the early evening till 1:00 a.m., and I think that first night we didn't even have sex. Pierre respected me, and I respected that. A white man who spoke Khmer—that was really something. I may not have loved Pierre, but I thought I could live with this man. He was simple, like a Cambodian. He ate rice and *prahoc* sauce. He lived like a Cambodian—he had a room with some other foreigners in a large wooden house, where the electricity often went off and the kitchen had a charcoal fire and a cold-water tap. Pierre wasn't rich, but of all the people I had ever met, he was the only one who was attentive to *me*— not to my body, but to me.

I told Pierre I wanted to get out of prostitution. I wanted to be clean, and decent. I hated selling my body to strangers. But I had no skills and very little money. He asked if I wanted him to help me set up a business, and the next morning he gave me a hundred dollars. He told me he wanted me to use it as a kind of start-up fund, to get a business going. He genuinely wanted to help me, and I was deeply touched by that.

I was also still shaken up from our conversation that first

night. Talking to Pierre brought back a lot of memories and a flood of emotion. I had told him about my adoptive family—how Father had tried to look after me in the village of Thlok Chhrov, how he'd registered me in school and how kind and good he was. When Pierre gave me the money, I suddenly thought again about how poor and tired Father had looked the day he caught sight of me riding in Dietrich's Land Cruiser. I decided to do something good for him.

I went out to the old Russian Market downtown and bought a stock of notebooks and pencils—small supplies that you could use to start a little shop. For a schoolteacher's family, it made sense to buy school supplies. But how could I get the supplies to my family? I would have to gather all my courage and go back.

In my memory, Thlok Chhrov was a place where people had always looked down on me. They hated me because I was just a savage. There were a few good people, and those are the ones I want to remember, but most of the villagers had only hard blows and insults for the dark-skinned kid who fetched them heavy pails of water every morning and worked for them in the fields. I knew that these people must now know I was a prostitute, for if Father had heard it, others most certainly had too. I knew they would look down on me, perhaps even throw stones. I didn't want to go back.

But I got onto a ferryboat that was headed for Kampong Cham. It wasn't very far—the trip took perhaps five hours—but all the way I was tense with nerves. I made sure I would arrive in Thlok Chhrov in the evening, when most people would be eating, so I wouldn't have to see anyone.

I hadn't been back since Phanna's wedding, in 1985, when I was a fifteen-year-old nurse in the rubber plantations of Chup. Now, over five years later, the village seemed somehow smaller, but richer too. Several houses had new shutters on their windows. There were even one or two big new houses made of solid wood planks. There was a second little shop standing beside the Chinese merchant's shop, where I'd first been raped. I felt a wave of hatred as I walked past.

The beaten-earth paths through the village were still the same, but Father's house was pitiful. The woven palm walls hadn't been changed for a long time. When we were children we were always having to weave new walls or new pieces of roof out of the long, dried coconut-palm leaves, but nobody had done that for a while. The house looked stained, worn, and black where insects and rot had eaten holes in the walls. It was sinking to one side, because the stilts were rotting. I felt a stab of guilt and pity.

They were home, the mother and father I had chosen for myself, or who had chosen me. They looked old and thin, and much smaller, like shriveled versions of themselves. When I came in they were eating from a small bowl of rice soup with a bit of dried fish in it, and I saw the surprise in their faces. But they didn't say very much. Father smiled and said, "Good to see you, Daughter."

I gave them the big bag of school supplies that I had bought with Pierre's money and explained clumsily what I had in mind. Mother smiled. I could see how relieved she was—it wasn't easy, living on a schoolteacher's meager pension. Unlike other schoolteachers in Cambodia, Mam Khon never demanded that his students pay him for the right to attend school or to pass exams. And because he was an honest man, he had very little money.

Mother made a fuss over me and apologized for not having more food. She offered to go out to the merchant to buy something, but I didn't want to embarrass her—I could see she had no money. And I didn't offer to go out to the merchant's shop myself.

Father had tears in his eyes, and Mother and I did too. We cried but we couldn't find any words. Memories were swirling around inside me—painful ones, and sweet. I couldn't tell these good people about my life in Phnom Penh, about being pawed and beaten and raped by a long succession of dirty and contemptuous men. My life was dishonorable and ugly, and I felt I was too.

They gave me news of Sochenda. She was living in Kampong Cham, the big local town, and working for the agriculture ministry in an office there.

Then Phanna came in. She was living in a shelter outside my parents' house—just a shack, really; it wasn't even on stilts. She worked as a schoolteacher in a nearby village. Her husband was out, but I gathered that he earned no money. All he did was feed the pigs and lie around the house. Phanna looked thin. She had somehow lost her looks—her pretty little mouth looked drawn and her eyes had lost their joy. She seemed far older.

Seeing how poor they had become made me want to help my family so much. Despite their poverty Father asked me again to come and live in the village with them. He said he wanted me to be "safe"—that was all that he said, but I understood what he meant and hung my head in shame. But I knew I couldn't come back to Thlok Chhrov. There was nothing there for me. It was a hateful little village, where very few people had been kind to me before; how much worse would they be to an ex-prostitute with no money? I shook my head.

I told Father I had met a man, a foreigner, who lived in

Phnom Penh. I said he seemed good and that he had given me the money to buy the school supplies. I knew that Father wouldn't like it, but I thought perhaps he would understand. A Khmer man would beat me and abuse me because I had been in a brothel. In Cambodia, I was forever stained. A foreigner might not mind so much about my past.

Father just asked me again to stay in the village. He said, "I don't want you to go back to the city. I'm afraid people will hurt you. Please stay here, at home."

I thought perhaps Father would force me to stay. The next morning, before daylight, I dressed and walked to the riverside in my city shoes and I took the dawn ferryboat back to Phnom Penh.

7

The French Embassy

When I returned to Guillaume's place in Phnom Penh I found a Cambodian man there waiting for me. He was the caretaker of the building where Pierre lived and he told me that Pierre was looking for me everywhere. I learned later that Pierre had even told a friend that he'd found the woman he was going to marry, the most beautiful girl he had ever seen, and he wasn't going to lose her so easily. He was crazy about me.

When I went to see him, Pierre asked me if I would like to move into his room in the large wooden house he shared in Phnom Penh with some other foreigners from humanitarian agencies. I was nervous about this. Pierre was poor and shabby—he wasn't the rich foreigner I'd had in mind. He wasn't like Hendrik, the rich American who lived in

Singapore who had once given me a hundred dollars just to spend on clothes. But Pierre spoke Khmer, and that really meant something to me. He was different from the other foreigners.

I asked Guillaume what he thought I should do, and he advised me to find somebody else. He said none of the foreigners much liked Pierre, that he was an arrogant loudmouth and I should bide my time. It wasn't much of a recommendation. Personally, I rather liked the fact that Pierre had a big personality, but I decided to do as Guillaume suggested.

Sometimes, when we were about to make love, Pierre would stop. He said he didn't want to force me. But I couldn't get the image of violence out of my mind. There was nothing I could do to annihilate my past. Coming back to life, to some kind of innocence, felt impossible. I didn't know where my youth was, where to dig to look—if not for happiness, then at least for a kind of peace. Pierre was kind, but for me, our nights together were always difficult.

Then Pierre left town, to go on vacation in Vietnam with some of his friends. I knew that these friends didn't think much of me. They thought I was unworthy trash he'd found on the street. One day, while Pierre was gone, I met a man I knew, a cousin of my adoptive mother. He was a big shot who worked in a government ministry and he asked me what I was doing in Phnom Penh.

I responded that I was a student—I was still attending the Alliance Française, so it wasn't quite a lie. My uncle invited me to have lunch with him, which I could hardly refuse. As we came out of the restaurant I saw a friend of Pierre's staring at me, so I stared back.

Pierre got back a few days later, and when I returned to his place I found a pile of my things on the floor. He was throwing me out. He told me I would always be a whore—he said that I had lied to him, that I didn't want to stop selling my body. He accused me of seeing clients while he was away.

It wasn't true. Since I'd met Pierre I hadn't slept with any other man. At that point, I still hadn't yet made up my mind about staying with him, but I wanted to show him that I respected him, as he showed respect for me.

When you're a whore, people always think you're dishonest. They assume you're a liar and a thief, and I always hated that. I would have left if Pierre had grown tired of me—that I would have accepted. But I hated that he could share the same opinion of me as everyone else—that he would think I was just a whore, a thief, a liar, a typical Phnong savage. I wanted him to see the kind of person I was trying to become, straight and honest.

I cried. I refused to leave. I told Pierre I had no ulterior motive in staying with him. I said I wasn't sleeping with him for money; there were plenty of wealthier men at Guillaume's house. And I hadn't chosen to be a prostitute. There was nothing at all voluntary in what I had done. I shouldn't be accused of sleeping with men when it wasn't the case. I asked him to give me the chance to prove I was not a liar.

It was while I was pleading with Pierre that I realized how much I wanted this. I wanted so badly to leave the world of prostitution behind me. Pierre was scruffy and sometimes strange and he got angry a lot, but he was different from anyone else. He spoke my language, and I thought that he understood me.

I vowed to myself that if Pierre took me back, I would stay with him and I would prove that I was more than just a prostitute.

We began living together. I didn't "love" Pierre. Sometimes I'm not even sure what the word means. But because Pierre spoke Khmer, it felt like we were a real couple—not like it was with Dietrich, strangers who nodded at each other and had sex when the male required it. I stopped going to the Alliance Française. We didn't have much money, and Pierre was teaching me a little French anyway.

In 1991 Pierre's contract with his humanitarian agency ended. He wanted to go back to France. I told him that if he left I wouldn't go to Europe with him, but that if he wanted to remain in Cambodia for a while, I would stay with him. He said he would stay—he would go back to France just for two weeks to do some business but he'd be back.

Pierre left me twenty dollars to tide me over. That was okay—it was enough for food. I spent a lot of time with the neighbors, a Cambodian family with two sweet little children. I didn't like sleeping alone with the whole apartment to myself, so at night the children used to come and stay over.

But Pierre didn't come back. It was three weeks, then four. Finally he phoned: he had been sick with malaria, but he was taking the plane the next day. When I went to get him at the airport I had forgotten what he looked like and I greeted the wrong man. I walked up to his friend Patrice— it's true they looked quite alike, but also I still had never looked Pierre straight in the eye. It took a long time for him to rid me of that old habit.

Pierre told me he didn't have another contract to work in Cambodia. Instead, he announced, he was going to set up a business. His idea was to open a bar overlooking the riverfront in downtown Phnom Penh. It was where all the new foreigners seemed to want to be—Phnom Penh was suddenly full of white people from the UN, who'd come to prepare the country to hold elections for a new government. Pierre said soon there would be peacekeeping troops from all over the place—like in Africa and Europe. He said you could bank on the fact that these people would be thirsty.

We moved in with a friend of Pierre's to save a little money while he looked for the right place. After a few months, he found an apartment on the first two floors of a building overlooking the river. Pierre wanted to make a little café out of it, a place you could go and have breakfast, with good coffee, but where you could also drink a beer in the evening and eat some food. He decorated it with palm leaves, like a village house, and put flowers everywhere. He called it "L'Ineptie"—"Nonsense." And it opened in 1992.

Pierre hired an Italian friend of his to make sandwiches and fondues and he took on four waiters. He waited on tables too, and so did I, sometimes till 2:00 a.m. I told Pierre I wasn't prepared to work for free, and he agreed to pay me twenty dollars a month. When I pointed out that this wasn't much, he told me I was getting free room and board.

Pierre invested all his money—a few thousand dollars—to get the place into shape. And at the end of the first month, he paid me. It was good, honest money. I went out to the market and spent it all on a sumptuous violet dress with a white lace collar and a little jacket. I thought I looked utterly beautiful in it! The Chinese man who sold it to me

for twice its value pulled a fast one on me, but I didn't want
to bargain. This little piece of happiness wasn't for bar-
gaining over. That evening, when I had stopped work, I
went up to the apartment and put my dress on again. I
never showed that dress to anyone, because I was too shy. It
was only for me—a magic gown that transformed everything.

One day Pierre telephoned his mother to say he had
split up with his former French girlfriend and was living
with me. She was horribly upset that he was living with a
Cambodian. I was disappointed; I hadn't realized French
people could be racist, just like the Khmer. But Pierre told
her, "I don't give a damn what you think." It shocked me to
hear him talk like that. How could he say "I don't give a
damn" to his own mother? In Cambodia, no matter how
old you are, you keep quiet in front of your parents and always show respect.

Pierre's friend Théo owned a video camera and he suggested we make a video to introduce me to Pierre's mother.
Pierre filmed me, but I was paralyzed with shyness. I
couldn't open my mouth and I doubt his mother warmed to
me much after watching it.

In those days, it never ceased to amaze me how much
French people talk. Cambodians are a silent people. We have
learned to stay mute the hard way. The French, on the other
hand, talked for hours when they hung out at L'Ineptie. I've
never seen people talk so much. I was exhausted just listening.

In November 1991 the prince returned to Cambodia. He
rode through Phnom Penh in the backseat of a pink
Chevrolet convertible, and children in the streets waved at
him. The return of the prince from exile was part of the

peace agreement that the United Nations had cobbled together for Cambodia. The Vietnamese agreed to withdraw
from their occupation of the country, Prince Sihanouk returned, the United Nations agreed to oversee the government and hold elections, and the guerrilla fighters—the
Khmer Rouge and all the other military units—agreed to try
to win those elections by all means possible.

Most of the Cambodians I knew were less than thrilled
by these developments. We have learned to be cautious;
when there is change in high places, this is often not good
news in low ones. When Khieu Samphan, a Khmer Rouge
leader, returned to Phnom Penh in late 1991 to open an
official office for the Khmer Rouge, a mob attacked him
and tore his office apart. Soldiers had to rescue him in a
tank. Most people feared that was just the beginning of the
trouble that the new election process would bring. Nobody
believed the fighters would turn in their guns and let the
country glide into a parliamentary democracy.

In 1992, twenty-two thousand foreigners arrived with
UNTAC, the UN peacekeeping force. Almost everyone welcomed this huge influx of *barangs*—as the Cambodians label
all white people—with their limitless money. New restaurants and bars opened almost every month in Phnom Penh
to service the foreigners' constant needs. A lot of them
were prostitute bars—places that were a little nicer than the
brothels—where the peacekeeping troops could go to pick
out girls. That business was booming, but there was no
prostitution at L'Ineptie.

If a foreigner turned up with a very young girl, as often
happened, Pierre would yell at him and throw him out. I
remember how angry he got one time when a big German
man came in with a girl of twelve or thirteen—I thought

there would be a fight. Perhaps that was why business wasn't very good. The place was often full, but mostly during the day, when people just hung out and talked.

I thought Pierre was brilliant. I admired him and if I ever thought of an ideal future it was to stay with him. He was a vehicle for me to escape my former life, to learn new ways to live in the world, and to be able to help my parents. I tried to love him too, and perhaps if he had been kinder that would have worked. But Pierre was rough, he yelled at me, he was not tender—it wasn't a fairy-tale romance.

By now I understood enough French to get by with the customers. Often the foreigners came in with Khmer who worked for them in the various nongovernmental organizations, UN agencies, and peacekeeping units. It was clear to me that these Khmer had a good life—nice clothes, and respect. I thought it would be good if I could learn enough French to be able to do that one day.

I sent money to my parents regularly. It was not money I took from Pierre—it was my own clean hard-earned money. One time I went back to Thlok Chhrov. My old friend Chettra drove me there on the back of her motorcycle. When we arrived, in the early evening, Father was in shorts, still beating the grains of rice out of a pile of rice stalks, though the light was fading fast. From Phanna's shack I could hear my sister crying out in pain and her baby son howling. I walked in—her husband was hitting her.

I told him to stop it. "Don't try to give me any lessons, whore," he said. I grabbed the chopping knife from the kitchen and made a gesture like I was going to cut his head in two, and he ran off.

Father probably intervened sometimes when Phanna was beaten. I'm sure it hurt him enormously to think that he had chosen such a bad husband for her. But it didn't change things much.

I told Phanna I thought she should get a divorce, but she said no. I have no idea whether or not she would have been the first woman in Thlok Chhrov to seek divorce, but to her it was unthinkable. I gave them money and returned to Phnom Penh with a heavy heart. A few months later I heard that she was pregnant with another child, her second.

A little later, Pierre hired a new waiter, a man I didn't like. He looked down on me because I was a Phnong, even though he knew I was with the boss. One time we had an argument and this waiter called me *"khmao,"* and I went to Pierre. I said he had to back me up, but Pierre said, "It's not my problem. You deal with it." I got angry and he actually hit me, right there, in front of the waiter. That was a real setback for me. I felt I could never really trust Pierre again. *Barang* or not, all men were alike.

For me, it's normal to work seven days a week, but Pierre found it exhausting to keep L'Ineptie going. He needed a break. One time he took me to Kep, on the coast, near where his friend Jean-Marc worked. They met there, talked and drank all night, and next morning slept till noon, like French people do. Then with more friends we took a boat out to Rabbit Island, just off the coast. We all slept at the house of an old woman on the island. It was beautiful: the full moon over the water, just like it was on the banks of the Mekong in Thlok Chhrov, with the woven crab traps bobbing on the surface of the sea.

The sea itself was unfamiliar, and I went in with all my clothes on, like a Cambodian woman. I couldn't even bear

to look at the other women with us, who were wearing biki-
nis. The water stung my skin—it was not like river water at
all—and it tasted salty. I wondered if people put salt into the
water. To make it easier for people to cook, perhaps?

Another time, Pierre said it was time for a real vacation.
He left L'Ineptie to a friend of his and told me we were going to Siem Reap to visit the thousand-year-old temples of
Angkor. I knew nothing about them, I only knew that the
silhouette of the Angkor Wat temple was printed on our
currency.

We took a boat out of Phnom Penh and moved upriver
to cross the great lake where the fishing people live out on
the water in movable, floating villages. The trip took all
night. In Siem Reap we stayed in a house rented by a friend
of Pierre's who worked for an NGO. The Cambodians who
owned the house were very nice to me. They didn't see me
as trash picked up from the street—they saw me as the com-
panion of a white man, somebody who deserved respect.

I was dumbstruck by Angkor Wat. The ruins were beautiful, but more moving to me was the way they were em-
braced and surrounded by thick forest. I had completely
forgotten the forest, the huge trees and leaves of my childhood in the hills of Mondulkiri. Here were vast palaces and
walkways with even vaster trees growing straight out of them,
broad and gnarled, with vines almost as high as you could
see, their roots making a towering frame around the carved
stone walls. I felt a sudden sense of recognition so strong I
could barely keep still. We couldn't go everywhere we
wanted to, because of the land mines, but I could tell that
the forest was deep and strong all around us.

We spent about fifteen days visiting the temples. Pierre

seemed to know all about them and lectured me on which king had built each one. I was amazed that I, a Cambodian, was so ignorant and he, a foreigner, was so knowledgeable. I asked him if he'd lived in Cambodia in a previous life. Pierre said that he had read books on Cambodian history and that if I could learn enough French I could read them too. I knew he thought it was a joke and that I would never be able to read *that* sort of French.

In Cambodia, there's nothing unusual about three people riding on one motorbike, and Pierre hired a man to drive us around. Sometimes we had to get off and push the motorbike through the rutted paths in the thick forest. We went as far as Banteay Srei, a small-scale temple in red stone about twelve miles into the forest. As we drove back down the paths through the forest, I plunged into distant memories and buried sensations. I asked Pierre to stop for a while. He quickly grew restless, but I would have stayed there forever, remembering what a forest sounds like, the noisy birdcalls and the cool, deep smells.

Pierre decided that we should make the journey back to Phnom Penh by plane. I had never gone up in a plane before, and I didn't trust the idea: I have never been able to understand how an airplane actually works. I spent the night thinking about it, eaten up by worry. By the time we got to the airport I was a complete mess, and when I saw the plane up close it looked like a metal bird—a tin can, some kind of joke. Pierre had to push me down into my seat and fasten my belt, which made me feel even more imprisoned. It felt like being tied down in the brothel. During takeoff and landing I was in a state of panic. When we arrived I was so green with nausea, I could barely stand up. I wondered if it is ever really possible to clear the past completely, or whether you will always be haunted by what has been done to you and what you have done.

In about February 1993, after L'Ineptie had been going for about a year, Pierre told me it wasn't making enough money. Neither he nor I had ever run a business, and I guess we weren't very good at it. And Pierre thought trouble was coming. The elections were being organized by the United Nations for May, and Pierre said nobody knew what would happen, whether the government would ever give up power and what kind of violence, even war, might flare up. Pierre said it was time for us to go to France.

I didn't feel ready for this huge new change, but at the same time, I wanted to see all the things Pierre had talked about. He said the world was much bigger than I had ever thought. I could already speak a little basic French, so I thought it wouldn't be too hard, and that if I went to France for a while I could come back and work as a translator or something. A lot of Cambodians were nervous about the political situation and would have leaped at the chance to get out. I could get a passport and a visa—but only if Pierre and I were married.

That's how we decided to take the plunge—as part of the visa process. I didn't want to get married at all. I don't even like the sound of the Khmer wedding music. To me marriage was like a chain, a prison. In Cambodia once you're married, your husband owns you.

After Pierre sold L'Ineptie he went to the French consulate to get all the forms we would have to fill out to be married and get visas. They all asked for my birth date, which of course I didn't know. I told Pierre it was sometime in 1970 and he wrote "1 April," because, he said, it was a kind of joke. It made me angry—I crossed it out and wrote "2 April" just to annoy him. I did the same thing with the date for our marriage to take place: Pierre wrote down "8 May," which is a French holiday, but it was also the date of Pierre's first, brief marriage to a Frenchwoman. That annoyed me too, so I struck it out and wrote in "10 May."

For my name I wrote "Somaly Mam." It was the truest name of all—Lost in the Forest—and anyway, Somaly was what Pierre called me. It had been years since anyone called me Aya, or just plain *khmao*. I called myself by the name my adoptive father gave me: his name, which I am proud to carry.

We went to the French embassy to be married. In those days the French embassy was an old colonial building with a red roof and jackfruit trees. It was impressive to be going there, but to me getting married was just part of the visa process. I didn't dress up or invite anyone. At the embassy I answered questions and said what Pierre told me to say and then we signed the papers. Pierre dealt with most of it.

Afterward Pierre's friend Thierry wanted us to have a little celebration. We ate in an Indian restaurant with some friends and then went to a nightclub that played mostly African music, for the Cameroonian peacekeeping troops. I remember how amazed people were when the first contingent of peacekeepers arrived from Cameroon, their skin so dark they looked like spirits. Pierre liked the music. He and his friends talked all night.

We left Cambodia a few days later. I took Pierre to Thlok Chhrov to see my parents and to talk to them. These days it was no problem to appear in the village in the broad light of day. Everything was different now that I was coming back to the village with money, and with a white man. Now everyone seemed to remember what close friends we had been as children, how sweet a child they'd always thought I was.

Father wasn't glad that I was leaving Cambodia, as I knew he would not be, and I don't suppose he was overjoyed to meet Pierre. He only nodded and said very little. I told him I would be back. My mother asked Pierre not to beat me, to love me and look after me; she asked him what my life would be like far away, in France. Pierre told them, "Don't worry, your daughter can look after herself." My parents both wept when we left.

Six days later we left for France. I had no idea what I might be getting into. A few days before we left, Pierre and I had a fight. When we left I was still seething with anger. I packed my suitcase and slipped a sharp knife inside it. If Pierre tries to sell me when we get to France, I said to myself, then I'll kill him. You never know.

8

France

In the airplane, I struggled to stay calm. I'm a proud person and I didn't want to show Pierre how frightened I was. We arrived in Malaysia, where we discovered that our second flight, to Paris, was delayed. The airline said they would put us up in a hotel.

To leave Kuala Lumpur Airport you had to use an escalator and I point-blank refused. There was no way I was going to step on this rolling metal serpent. Pierre was exasperated—he had to tug me onto it. In the streets I saw buildings higher than the tallest trees in the forest. Pierre said they were skyscrapers, and I thought he must mean it literally. Everything astonished me—it was all so modern.

Our hotel room was on the twenty-eighth floor, and to get there we had to take the elevator. When the doors

closed, it felt like being in a coffin, shut in and panicky.
From our hotel room the people down below looked tiny,
like insects. I was terrified. Pierre went into the bathroom
and ran a bath full of bubbles. He told me I would like it,
that I should get in, but I wouldn't do it. I had never taken
a bath before or washed in hot water and I was afraid of the
bubbles.

Then there was another plane. I was more blasé about
the flight by now, though it was longer, and we stopped in
Dubai. At the Dubai airport I saw how Muslims live—not
the Cham like Grandfather was, but the real ones, with the
women covered all in black like ghosts, shut away inside
their own clothes, so close and hot in such a hot country. I
felt sorry for them.

When we arrived in France we went straight to the house
of Pierre's Aunt Jeanine, in the suburbs of Paris. When we
walked outside in the crisp May air I thought they had
somehow put air-conditioning outdoors. To please me,
Aunt Jeanine had decided to cook rice. In Cambodia we
cook rice for an hour or more on coals, and it simmers
slowly. When I saw her plunging little plastic packages into
boiling water, I thought she was mad, and even more when
after a few minutes she took it out and added butter. It
looked awful, half boiled, half raw: swollen and much fat-
ter than our rice, which is nutty and fragrant. Out of respect for the rice seedlings, I ate it all. I loved the ham,
though, and the bread—the bread was marvelous.

Then Pierre took off for a couple of days. He said he
had to go and see some friends and he disappeared. Jeanine
was out most of the day, and I didn't know what to do. I
was too unsure of my few French words to go out, and I was
afraid of getting lost. I thought perhaps my friends were

right—Pierre did have plans to sell me. I told myself I had to be strong; I had to show Pierre what I was made of.

Finally, on his return, Pierre suggested that we visit Paris. We were in a distant suburb and had to take the train and then the metro. All these things were new to me, incomprehensible and disturbing. In Cambodia trains move at the speed of a walking man. This train raced at dizzying speed along two thin rails, looking as if it might slip off at any moment, and the metro was underground, hurtling through the dark earth lightning fast.

I had heard that Paris was the most beautiful city in the world, but I didn't think so. There was hardly any green, and the city seemed choked and dead, with buildings tightly packed together. There was no space anywhere. Even the celebrated Eiffel Tower didn't thrill me—it looked like a pile of old iron, nothing like the splendor or power of Angkor Wat. The most surprising thing was to see how people behaved with their dogs. There were dogs inside restaurants and apartments. Cambodian dogs live outside—to us, they're dirty animals.

I also watched people getting money out of a sort of big box in the wall. So that's how they do it, I said to myself. When they need it, people just go and fetch money from the box—what a good idea. I folded a piece of paper and slipped it into the slot. Nothing happened. Pierre laughed and explained about bank cards and the whole system, which seems extraordinary to me even today.

We went to stores and saw masses of pointy shoes. My Cambodian clothes looked dismal in comparison.

We were invited to dinner at the house of Pierre's Uncle Jean. Pierre had warned me that his family was rather conservative. Jean came to fetch me in a nice car—Pierre was

somewhere else—and put his seatbelt on. He gestured for
me to do the same, but I shook my head to show I didn't
understand. I pulled the seatbelt when he showed me, but
he had to latch it for me. When we arrived at his house,
Jean got out and closed his door. I was still in the car and
had no idea how to unfasten the belt. He mimed the action,
but I didn't know what to do, so he had to unfasten me
himself.

I felt I had not just failed a test, I didn't even know what
the test was. At dinner the food was a mystery. Some of it
was simply revolting. Fish in cream sauce that I had to force
myself to swallow. I thought the cheeses smelled horrible.
The French seemed to eat vast quantities of everything, especially meat. I could hardly believe how much they seemed
to put inside themselves every day.

I was overcome by it all: the succession of dishes, the
abundance of food, and the fact that people left food on
their plates. They cut off the fat and left it; they left meat
around the bones and didn't even suck them; then they
cheerfully threw it all away, along with the thick fish skin.
We would have fed whole families in Cambodia just with
these leftovers. In Thlok Chhrov we only ate meat once or
twice a year, on special holidays. My mother would buy a
half pound of pork for twenty people and chop it up very
fine, as a kind of flavoring. We were grateful for every grain
of rice we got.

That dinner went on for a long time. At one or two in
the morning, everyone was still talking. Pierre didn't translate anything for me. I was lost, jet-lagged, and hungry because I couldn't eat the food. Everyone smiled at me, but
there was no contact at all. I was Pierre's little foreign sav-

age, sitting at the end of the table without uttering a single word.

We went to Nice to visit Pierre's mother. She had a yappy little dog, Tatou, who barked the whole time and ate from a plate at the table, which I found truly disgusting. The plan was for us to live with Pierre's mother for a while, until Pierre found a job, but I could tell that she didn't like me. To her I was a gold-digging foreigner who had seduced her son, and I tried to stay out of her way. Pierre was out most of the time, and I just sat in our room with no one to talk to and nothing to do.

I desperately needed to take French lessons, but we didn't have much money. I had brought a French-Khmer dictionary with me from Cambodia and I asked Pierre to recommend a children's book for me to read. Pierre told me I'd never manage it, but he bought me a copy of Joseph Kessel's *Le Lion*. He was right—it was far too difficult for me. But I told myself I had to do it, and every night I wrote down words I had to learn.

Pierre went off to Paris to look for work while I stayed behind in Nice with his mother. One day I found a copy of the local paper, *Nice-Matin*. Looking through it, I came upon the classified section. I saw the word *"Emploi"* and looked it up in the dictionary—it meant "jobs." I translated a few ads with the aid of my dictionary, and I saw that people were looking for cleaners and maids. I realized that even with little French, I might be able to find work.

I asked my mother-in-law how to get a job, and she took me to a temp agency and dropped me off. She didn't care to help me, so I just walked in by myself. There were all kinds of foreigners inside. I explained to the director that I wanted to work. I told him, *"Je veux travailler,"* in a loud voice, and he got the message. He smiled broadly and told me I could start the next morning. I would be a cleaner at the Hôtel Hibiscus on the Promenade des Anglais.

That night, when Pierre phoned from Paris, I told him I had found work. He couldn't believe it—that I would find a job before he could, without even speaking proper French. I was so happy about the salary. With 2,500 francs a month, I thought, I could begin sending money home to my parents.

The next morning my mother-in-law drove me to the hotel, and I carefully memorized the route into the center of town. When I arrived a Madame Josiane met me and gave me a dozen rooms to clean. She didn't show me how, and I had no idea how to make a bed properly. I also didn't know how to use the vacuum cleaner. It was like a long snake and roared at me—I was always frightened that it would suck up my feet or climb up my body. I had to make a great inner effort to control my fear of it. I was also puzzled by the variety of cleaning products.

That first day I didn't even try to use the vacuum cleaner and I made the bed all wrong. When Madame Josiane came back she said, "Oh la la," and laughed, and showed me how to do it, using sign language. By the end of the day, I could tell she was pleased with my work. I cleaned behind and under the furniture without being told, and I didn't stop for lunch, as the other cleaners did—I didn't even stop work to drink. And I never minded working weekends.

At the end of the month I got my first paycheck. I had only been in France for two months and I'd already earned

2,500 francs, a huge sum of money. In Cambodia that would be a fortune, perhaps a year's pay. But what was I to do with this piece of paper, a check? Pierre explained that he would open a joint bank account for us, and I should deposit it there. That made me nervous. What if we divorced? Pierre could take all my money. I told him that I wanted to open an account in my own name, and he said, "You're a real Chinese woman."

I don't have a habit of trusting men, and I never really trusted Pierre. Soon after we got to Nice, he went to see his ex-wife and didn't come back until five in the morning.

Sometimes the hotel clients tipped me. I remember one elderly woman: after I helped her put away her clothes, she took my face in her hands and said, *"Mignonne."* I didn't know the word and asked her to write it down so that I could look it up in my dictionary. She thought I was pretty! I looked at myself in the mirror and thought she must be making fun of me.

After a couple of months of working at the Hôtel Hibiscus I realized that I could make more money at another hotel. The Hibiscus paid badly, and I had to work seven days a week. Also, some of the male hotel clients bothered me. I suppose they saw me as a little Asian girl who wouldn't make a fuss. I didn't want to put up with that kind of thing anymore and now I knew I didn't have to.

I went to work at another hotel. The clientele there was mainly retired people who stayed for several weeks at a time. This gave me the chance to get to know them a little, and those elderly people were the ones who really taught me French. Some of them were very kind: they called me their "little Chinese princess." I saw that French people lump all Asians together, but I didn't mind it—Cambodians do the same with foreigners; to us they're all *barang*.

I like old people. They deserve to be looked after with respect. Sometimes, if their bones ached, I would rub their legs and massage their ankles. They appreciated that. They began joking with the hotel management that the pretty, pleasant girl was cleaning bedrooms while all the disagreeable staff members waited tables in the restaurant. So I was told to clean rooms only in the morning; at lunch I would wait tables.

I got lots of tips, but that made all the other staff jealous. They called me "Chink." My orders were never cooked on time. Finally, after a few weeks, I cracked. I grabbed a knife in the kitchen and shouted at one girl, "If you keep going I'll stick this in your belly." I was surprised to realize that I knew how to say it. It didn't make me any friends, but it brought me peace. After that they left me alone.

My mother-in-law was still hostile. I cleaned for her, and sometimes I offered to cook, but she didn't like my food and never spoke to me much. It was always clear that she would prefer to be alone with her son—she constantly tried to drive a wedge between us. When I got home after work in the afternoons, I didn't dare make myself lunch, even though I was always hungry.

I lost a lot of weight. One time she fed Pierre and me eggs and spinach and gave meat to her dog. I put up with everything, because according to Cambodian custom you have to put up with everything your mother-in-law does and not complain to your husband. A Khmer husband will always take his mother's side against his wife, so it's best to endure in silence.

But after we had lived in Pierre's mother's apartment for four months, some friends of hers came to visit. They had children with them—the kind who jump on everything and destroy stuff. I said to one of the little ones, "Don't jump about like that. When the old lady comes back she won't be happy." To me this wasn't any kind of insult. In Cambodia we say *"yeh"* for any elderly woman—it's a term of respect. But in Europe nobody wants to face facts; you have to pretend they're not old, even if they're elderly. When my mother-in-law got home, the mother of the little monsters told her I'd called her "the old lady," and my mother-in-law was furious. She slapped me and locked me in my room.

She might have thought about how little French I could speak; she could have tried to understand. I was horribly upset. I explained everything to Pierre when he got back. To my surprise, he understood immediately and said it was time for us to find another place to live.

Pierre had just found a temporary job as a lab technician, which made paying the rent easier. We rented a one-room studio on the ground floor of an apartment building, with a little garden outside. The first night I had a nightmare: the garden was squirming with slugs, like the maggots Aunty Peuve's guards used to throw on my face and body. I screamed uncontrollably. Pierre was horrified, but I spent the rest of the night wearing socks, several pairs of pajama bottoms, gloves, and a hat. I didn't want any of those slugs to touch me.

But those nightmares were growing rare. The Central Market in Phnom Penh was far away, and I was starting to get used to a new life. One afternoon I left work early and decided to explore the city of Nice, which I barely knew. I took the bus. I got off at a bus stop at random and walked

around in an area I didn't know. I got lost and phoned
Pierre, but he told me to work it out myself, like a big girl—
if I'd gotten there, I could always get back.

Since the place where we lived was close to the sea, I told
myself that if I walked along the coast I'd manage to find my
way home. I walked until my feet ached, and when I looked
up I saw a sign written in Khmer. *Ku tieu Phnom Penh*—Noodle
soup, Phnom Penh style. I thought I was dreaming. I went
in and started speaking to the people in Khmer. They responded. I was overwhelmed and tears came to my eyes. I sat
down and drank two bowls of good, spicy soup. Then I had
a coffee with condensed milk poured onto ice cubes, the
way we drink it in Cambodia.

This is how I made contact with the Khmer community
in Nice. The owners of the restaurant said they had a
Khmer group and were planning a small festival with Cambodian Apsara dances to celebrate the New Year in April. I
had learned those dances as a child in Thlok Chhrov, and
they asked me to join the performance.

Then Pierre's contract as a lab technician ended—it was
only temporary, and it wasn't renewed. I was earning about
3,000 francs a month at the hotel, but our one-room
apartment alone cost us 2,500. Pierre had met someone
who wanted to start up a medical analysis laboratory in
Cambodia, but the negotiations were dragging out. I
needed to find work and now knew that there were a lot of
Asian restaurants along the coast.

I knocked on all kinds of doors. A Chinese man from
Cambodia agreed to give me a job in his restaurant, washing up. He even said that I could eat rice there before starting work. I wouldn't be working officially—he didn't want to

pay employee charges to the state—but I was just glad to have the money.

Sometimes I got paid, sometimes I didn't. I used to leave the apartment at six in the morning, walk six miles to the hotel and work there till three in the afternoon, come home at four, then leave at six to go to the restaurant. Pierre would come and get me at one or two in the morning. He always complained that I smelled of the kitchen, and finally I told him I'd walk home alone.

Pierre was never a comforting man—he's no good at tenderness. He's straightforward, and his angles are sharp and sometimes cut. There were advantages to this. Pierre taught me to fend for myself, and he made me speak up—he hated it when I was mute.

One summer day at the hotel, I fainted. The doctor said it was overwork and told me to take a two-week break. But I don't know how to do nothing, and two days later, I was back. The truth is, I enjoyed working at the hotel. I liked looking after elderly people—they seemed to care for me.

After the summer rush was over, the hotel informed me that it was my turn to take a vacation. I had worked for a year, and according to my pay stubs I had accrued four weeks of leave. I had never gone on "vacation" before—I had no idea you had a right to such a thing, and I couldn't imagine doing what the French people did in Nice. They mostly walked around in colorful clothes and spent money, it seemed to me. We didn't have any, so that wasn't an option.

A cousin of my mother-in-law's suggested we could get

temporary work doing the *vendange*—the grape harvest. He told us he knew a man who could give us work in Ville-franche, harvesting Beaujolais grapes for a month. Pierre thought it would give us some fresh air and a change of scenery, so we went.

Monsieur Marcel was nice enough about it, but when he saw me he said, "She'll never make it." I was just a little thing—I weighed about ninety pounds, and he was at least double that. But I told Pierre, "He'll see." I was used to physical work.

Pierre couldn't bear the cold, the humidity, the earth that stuck to his feet. He just couldn't do the work, but I loved it. It was beautiful to be outdoors and smell the earth, feel grapes in my hand, and I thought cutting grapes was a lot easier than harvesting rice. Pierre was proud of me, and so was Monsieur Marcel. He used to call me "our little Chink," but he meant it in the nicest possible way.

At set hours, we all stopped to take a break and eat. That's where I learned to eat cheese and cold sausage—in other words, to become altogether French. I discovered really good country cooking, soups and tasty dishes far better than the plastic sachets of rice I'd had in Paris. Monsieur Marcel and his family were really good people. After the harvest was done there, I wanted to continue, so we went to Gevrey-Chambertin in Burgundy. The manager there was so pleased with me that he gave me a bottle of wine to take home.

But in spite of this good work, we had decided to leave France and return to Cambodia. Pierre had found another job there, with another humanitarian agency. This time he would be working for Médecins Sans Frontières, Doctors Without Borders. Pierre had concluded that he wasn't made for life in France—it just didn't agree with him. He wanted adventure, something less settled than a small medical analysis lab in Nice.

I was proud to be going back home. I knew that I had changed a lot during the eighteen months we'd been living in France. I had worked honest jobs. I had learned to look people in the eye and communicate with them directly, as an equal. I knew that when I went back to Cambodia people would no longer look down on me as a white man's whore. They would see me as a white man's *wife*. I was like the people we call Khmers de France—Cambodians who live in France and come back on holiday with money and power and with the white person's sense of self-assurance. I might have dark skin and I might still look like a savage, but I had proved that I wasn't stupid, and I no longer felt worthless.

9

Kratie

Pierre's new job was in Kratie, an old colonial town on a bend of the Mekong River, about two hundred miles northeast of Phnom Penh. In November of 1994 we moved into a room in a big house near the river that was rented by several people who worked for Médecins Sans Frontières. Almost all the white MSF team members lived together—it was cheaper that way, and they paid a Cambodian woman to come in to clean and cook.

Pierre didn't want to pay the extra for the cook—he said it was too expensive, and anyway, he didn't want to spend all his time talking to other French people. This was what Pierre was like: if we were in Cambodia, he wanted to live like a local. I liked that attitude. He would rather eat rice at roadside stalls with the Cambodian staff members of MSF than share roast chicken with the doctors.

Still, there was a good atmosphere at the MSF house. I used to help the cook clean up. She was an older woman, about fifty, and her name was Veasna, but everyone called her Yvonne because that was easier. At first she was surprised that I helped her. She thought that because I was a Khmer de France I would think I was superior. I told her I wasn't really a Khmer de France, but I didn't tell her anything about my past.

I went to see my adoptive parents soon after we arrived. We met in Kampong Cham, which was not too far away; my sister Sochenda was living there, and I wanted to see her and her new baby. Sochenda had married a man of her own choice. After she got her graduation certificate she went to a training college in Kampong Cham and she married a fellow student there. I had heard that both of them were now working in the agriculture ministry.

I was shocked by their living conditions. The house Sochenda and her husband lived in with their two children, and now a third, was pitiful. They were really poor—Sochenda had recently stopped working, because their salaries hadn't been paid for so long—and they had just been burglarized and had lost most of the things they owned.

Then Phanna arrived, and I was shocked again when I saw her—she was thin and old, not pretty and young anymore. She had brought her five-year-old son with her and her daughter, Ning, a beautiful little girl who was three and a half.

Then my parents arrived, both of them on the back of

an ancient motorcycle taxi, looking thin and shriveled. They all looked so sad, and when they saw one another everyone began crying. I felt a rush of love and pity for them—they had never complained when they had written to me in France. They had always said everything at home was fine and never once asked me for money as most families would.

I thought to myself, I know why I'm back, it is to look after these people. This family had held out its hand to me and taken me in, these people were everything I had, and I would never abandon them again.

Sochenda had nothing in the house to eat, not even rice—just a couple of sweet potatoes—and her boys were thin. I went out and bought a hundred-pound sack of rice and all kinds of food: chicken, and fish to make fish soup. I bought a lot, but they ate it all. They were so hungry they could hardly restrain themselves.

I stayed two nights. The first night Father asked me if I wanted to go to a hotel and I said no. I might have been to France, but I was still the same person—I told him my name was still Somaly, the name he gave me when I was a child in Thlok Chhrov. But the truth is I was shocked at how dirty everything was. I was no longer used to washing under a sarong using the outside shower, and the bed was unbelievably uncomfortable. I had changed.

When I got back to Kratie, I told Pierre I wanted to help my family. He said, "It's your money, do what you want." I gave them money to buy supplies, to set up a business selling things. My parents had lived for a long time off the hundred dollars in school supplies that I had given them. Long before it became a saying, my father always used to tell us in Thlok Chhrov, "It is better to give a fishing net than a fish."

During the day I often went to the government clinic where Médecins Sans Frontières had set up operations. I helped out with translation, because most of the MSF team didn't speak any Khmer. One day a traditional healer was brought in. He was protesting—he didn't want to go to the government hospital—but two younger-looking people had brought him in, and he was too weak to resist. The doctors called me because he needed treatment but didn't want to take it.

When I asked if I could help, the old man began talking to me in his own language.

I realized that he recognized me in some way and I also realized that I could more or less understand the gist of what he was saying. Maybe his language resembled the one spoken in my forest, I don't know. But I started thinking about my childhood again for the first time in a long time—remembering what it was like. I had forgotten Phnong. That night I couldn't sleep. I realized I had forgotten where I came from and who I was.

Now that we were back in Cambodia, I had to decide what to do. Money didn't matter to me—we had enough. I asked Pierre's boss at the Médecins Sans Frontières clinic if I could work as a volunteer there every morning. After all, I had been more or less trained as a midwife in Chup—as trained as anyone was, in those days, in Cambodian hospitals. And I could speak French and Khmer, which in and of itself was useful.

I began working in the clinic every morning as an assistant, in the team that treated sexually transmitted diseases. I worked with a fat nurse whom I didn't like much. Behind the doctors' backs, she was always telling the patients that they had to pay her for the medical care, even though it wasn't true. I applied treatments, washed wounds, and helped clients understand how to look after themselves. They had gonorrhea, chancres, genital warts.

Most of the people who came to the clinic were men. Some of them looked shamefaced, but most of them just seemed angry. I hated them. I knew they got these diseases by buying and raping prostitutes. But I wanted them healed, because I knew they were also infecting those prostitutes and their wives, so I looked after them.

One day a girl came in. She was about eighteen years old, and I saw immediately that she was a prostitute—you could tell right away. I also knew that she would lie about it. What "broken woman" could go to a respectable hospital in Cambodia and be treated properly?

I saw how my colleague dealt with her, hostile and scornful, and I took her aside and spoke to her very gently. I explained the treatment and talked to her about sexually transmitted disease. I said she should try to keep clean and use condoms and I told her about HIV infection. AIDS had been around in Europe for over a decade, but in 1994 the epidemic had only recently begun in Cambodia. (Today, we have one of the highest rates of AIDS infection in Asia.)

I told that girl to tell the others that, if they needed treatment, they could come to the clinic any morning. I would be there, and I would see that they were treated well. After that, girls from the brothels began coming into the clinic in small groups. They were sixteen, seventeen, twenty-one years old. They weren't children, but they were young. Some of them looked at me with sweetness and a kind of hope, but most of them looked at me with resignation and a great deal of pain.

I knew these girls: they were me. I knew exactly what their lives were like. I found it was no longer possible for me to sleep at night back in the Médecins Sans Frontières house by the river. Every night I thought about those girls leaving the hospital, sick, going back to the places where that same evening they would be beaten and raped by clients.

I felt I didn't have a choice: I needed to help them get out of the life they were imprisoned in, just streets away from me. This was something I could do that few other people could.

I knew where the girls would be because I knew my way around their world, and I knew how to communicate with them. The words themselves weren't as important as the bond between us. When a victim meets another victim, there's a look of understanding that is very powerful. I was connected to these girls, and they trusted me. I had to help them.

Most of them told me they had no soap to wash with, and I knew that was true: I had never had soap. They told me that if their clients did use condoms, they were cheap Thai ones in all kinds of strange shapes that used to tear all the time. So I started there. I talked to Pierre's boss at MSF and asked him to give me a stock of condoms that I could distribute to prostitutes, and I asked for dozens of bars of soap. I argued that they might not be medical supplies, but they were important for preventing illness too.

He sighed—it was difficult for MSF to do this kind of thing, because it's an organization that focuses on emergency humanitarian relief, not preventive work for sexually transmitted disease. Still, I don't know how, but he got me a supply of condoms and an information pack about preventing HIV. He said he drew the line at buying me bars of soap—I would just have to manage on my own.

I went out to the market and bought soap. Then, rather than distributing the condoms and soap only at the hospital, to girls who were already sick, I began to go to the brothels and give them out there, to everybody. I thought this made more sense.

The brothels in Kratie were not like the brothels in Phnom Penh. They weren't in clapped-out buildings near the marketplace: these were little shanties, on stilts, in the muddy garbage by the river, on the outskirts of town. But in every other respect they were just as dirty and just as brutal as the brothels I'd known. Walking toward them I would start to sweat, but I kept going, even though being there made me want to vomit.

I used to pretend to be a nurse from Médecins Sans Frontières. I dressed like a Khmer de France and came in with an official air and a box of condoms. I told the meebons that I wanted to help keep the girls healthy, and that it was for the best that the girls be free of disease. They could only agree. Also, I think they were a little afraid of me: a Khmer de France, the wife of a white foreigner. They didn't dare prevent me from coming in.

The first morning I found one girl who was so small I thought she must be aged about twelve, though she said she was sixteen. A client had torn off her nipple, and the wound was infected. I told the meebon she should let me take the girl to the hospital to be treated. That turned out to be easy: it was in the *meebon*'s interest to keep her slaves in good condition, and this way she didn't have to spend a cent.

I sat with the girl in the clinic and made sure the nurses treated her properly. She was cheerful and grateful, and my heart ached that evening when I had to take her back.

That happened a few more times, and I realized that I could do this more often. You can't look at a girl who's badly hurt and not want to get her help. If I managed to get the girls back to the brothels by evening, in time for work, the *meebons* would let me bring them to the hospital in a taxi.

I asked Médecins Sans Frontières to let me have a car and driver so I could bring some of the sickest girls to the clinic every morning. In frustration, when it looked as though MSF wouldn't help me, I took the wife of Pierre's boss to the brothels so she could see the situation for herself. Her name was Marie-Louise. She was a doctor too and a really good woman. She saw the battered girls in scummy places, their wounds and scars, and she was horrified. She couldn't believe how people treated other human beings. By the time we came back to the MSF office, she was speechless. From that point on Marie-Louise made sure that I'd have the use of a car.

France had changed me. I was not afraid of people anymore. I began spending most of the day in the brothel neighborhoods of Kratie. It wasn't just about distributing condoms and information about HIV or about ferrying girls to the hospital. It was about being close to these girls and connecting with them in a deeper way.

When I was in Aunty Peuve's brothel, there were many

times I needed someone to help me—even just someone who would put her arms around me when I cried. For me there had been no one, though I was lucky in other ways. Now I needed to be that person for others.

The girls in Kratie were mostly debt slaves, as I once was. They were paying back a loan taken out by their parents or relatives. Some of them had agreed to do it. This is Cambodia: If you are a girl, you owe obedience to your parents. If your family requires you to sell your body on the side of the road so that your younger brother can go to school—or so your mother can gamble—that is what you do. You don't feel like you have a choice.

A few of the girls had been sold outright. Those were the ones who lived in the nastiest places, where the owners were more hostile and the brothel more heavily guarded, and many of the girls were very young. They were captives, and I couldn't take them out to the hospital. But other brothels were not as heavily guarded.

The pimps know their livestock won't try to escape. A girl's will is easily broken and she quickly learns she has nowhere to run. They couldn't go back to their homes because they were no longer welcome there. They were broken. They had no skills, no way to support themselves on their own. They were condemned to sell themselves more or less forever. I felt the panic of it, the echo of my own experience.

The first girl I helped escape was dark skinned, like me. She had straight hair all the way down her back. She was sixteen, and she had been a prostitute for over a year. She was guarded, but I had to help her.

I found a tailor in Sambo, a village about ten miles up the river from Kratie. It wasn't far, but I hoped it would be far enough. This woman was willing to take girls in and train them as seamstresses for one hundred dollars each. I asked Pierre for the money, and he gave it to me. To his great credit, Pierre almost never complained about this kind of thing, no matter how much I spent.

I went back to the brothel and told the *meebon* this girl had to come to the clinic the next day for more treatment. But when we were alone together, I told the girl not to come. I didn't trust the fat nurse, my colleague—she liked money too much. I said we should meet at my house and I would take her to the village. When the *meebon* and her guards came to the clinic looking for her, nobody had seen her, and my fat colleague told the guards she must have escaped—this happens sometimes. They went away.

Sambo was far enough away to escape their notice. I paid for two more girls, then another two—I sent them to learn sewing from this seamstress and I gave them a small living allowance. I wasn't buying them out of prostitution, because I didn't have that kind of money. But I was giving them a way out, if they could manage to leave.

I had been doing this for a couple of months when one of the pimps in the neighborhood put a gun to my head. I knew him. He was an old man called Mr. Eng. The prostitutes in this old man's brothel were heavily guarded, and he never let them out. I hadn't encouraged any of his girls to leave.

I was going to Mr. Eng's brothel to give out condoms and talk, but before I'd begun climbing up the ladder to his stilt house, he stepped out of the chair where he'd been dozing in his undershirt, a gun in his hand. He held it against my head and told me to get out or he would shoot me.

I just looked at him. I don't know where I got the courage, but I said, "If you kill me, then your wife, your

children—all of you will go to prison, because I am protected. You know who I am. All of you will be killed."

I was a Khmer de France and a white man's wife. He put
the gun down.

When I told Pierre about it later, he said I should go to
the police station to file a proper complaint, like a foreigner would do. I discovered that the provincial police
chief was the brother of Yvonne, the woman who cooked
and cleaned at the MSF team's house. Mr. Eng was taken
into custody very quickly after that, and I had no more
trouble for a while.

I knew that what was needed was a place for prostitutes to
live and be looked after once they managed to escape.
Pierre's salary wasn't limitless, and I knew just how many
more girls there were. I also thought that, with money,
there might be some way to rescue the girls who were captives. They would need somewhere safe to live—somewhere
the pimps wouldn't get them. They needed training. I
started to write down notes, in Khmer, about what I
thought this should look like—I was thinking of some kind
of charity that could collect funds.

Then I began feeling ill. It never occurred to me that I
might be pregnant. To be safe, I was also taking birth control pills. When I realized why I had been feeling so terrible, I panicked.

I didn't want children. They are so vulnerable. They feel
so much pain, and it is impossible to protect them. I felt I
would never know how to look after a child properly, because I had never had a mother. But Pierre was delighted.

He told me, "Nature will look after you." It was a little un-realistic, but sweet.

Pierre began helping me with my idea for a charity to help prostitutes. He and his Dutch friend Eric Merman, who worked with MSF, started writing the organization's charter. Then Pierre landed a new job in Phnom Penh, with an American relief agency. He would be earning a lot more money and he told me he'd decided to accept.

10

New Beginnings

I found us a two-bedroom house on the outskirts of Phnom
Penh, in a neighborhood called Tuol Kok. Houses were
cheaper there and they had yards, but it wasn't one of the
places the white foreigners had started moving to—it was
a Cambodian neighborhood. I had no idea it was a center
for brothels, but I realized soon enough. Right near our
house was a brothel they called the "Broken Coconut"—
"coconut," in Khmer, is another word for a woman's secret place. The *meebon* stood outside it, shouting at the girls
if they didn't look lively enough. They were so young. I
didn't see a girl older than about nineteen; many were as
young as twelve.

All along the main road heading toward the city, for almost a mile, were filthy shacks where girls with painted faces beckoned men on the roadside. These girls were mostly for local use: they were for *motodup* drivers, construction workers, laborers. But there were also a number of brothels on that road that were more specialized. They offered younger children. Cambodians called it Antenna Street after the tall radio-transmitter tower, but foreigners had begun calling it *"la rue des petites fleurs"*—the street of little flowers—because there were so many young girls for sale.

A few days after we moved in to Tuol Kok, a young policeman came by to register us as new residents. This was still the system in those days, and since Pierre was foreign, I suppose we merited a special home visit. The policeman, named Srena, was a young boy, about nineteen, and he looked hungry. I served him tea and some fish soup, and he told me a little about himself.

I was about six months pregnant, but I couldn't just sit at home doing nothing. I'm not that kind of person. And it was impossible to ignore the misery of the brothels that were all around me. I began distributing condoms, just as I had in Kratie, and taking girls to the clinic—I pretended to be a health worker from Médecins Sans Frontières, which was not a great idea, but I didn't have a better one.

I had to steel myself to go back into the dank, filthy alleyways behind the Central Market where I used to work. I never did manage to force myself to go back to the place where Aunty Peuve's brothel had been. It was too alive with memories—it made me feel ill to go near it.

I don't know if people recognized me on the street. Probably not. I was dressed differently, and I had a completely different air about me. Who would connect a self-assured, well-dressed pregnant woman to the dismal, scrawny ghost called *"khmao"*? I didn't go looking for anyone I knew—I was pretty sure everyone was gone.

Phnom Penh had changed enormously in just two and a half years. It was far richer, far more crowded. There were building sites everywhere. The brothels had changed too. Aunty Peuve's brothel had been hidden, like the other establishments, in alleyways behind the main street; now they were right out front. They were official.

The worst places, without question, were in Svay Pak. We had a car—a rattling pale-blue Camry that Pierre had bought for eight hundred dollars—and I used to drive there. Six miles out of the city, it was a whole neighborhood of brothels, clustered around the main road. In Svay Pak there were shacks, but there were also other brothels in concrete houses with high gates and walls. They looked like fortresses, and it was obvious that the people inside were armed: every business in Phnom Penh had a weapon. Most of these places wouldn't let me in. Many of the girls inside were captives and some of them were very young children. Svay Pak specialized in ethnic-Vietnamese girls, pale and beautiful, virgins.

Some of the children were ten years old, sometimes younger. I had never seen that before, and it shook me. They were often badly hurt. I began my daily routine: going out to the brothels every day and bringing girls for treatment to the MSF clinic or to the hospital where Pierre worked.

Phanna's daughter, Ning, was very sick. She was about five years old, and since they'd moved to Phnom Penh she'd been ill. Pierre and I took her to the hospital, and she was diagnosed with tuberculosis. She was hospitalized. She came out of the hospital, but she was still convalescing when Phanna came to see me one day, white as a sheet.

She told me her husband was planning to give Ning to a neighbor, a woman who had offered to take Ning in, since she had no children—she had even offered him money. He said that since Ning was always sick anyway, this was a good solution. Phanna came and begged me to find a way out, and so, when I was eight months pregnant, Pierre and I decided to have Ning come and live with us. She was the sweetest child in the world, a truly endearing little girl, and we already adored her anyway.

The time was coming for me to give birth, but I was still uneasy at the idea of having a child. There was a creature growing inside me who moved and kicked and soon would need me, but I felt paralyzed by the thought of being a mother to someone. I had never had a mother and I painfully felt that hole in my life. To be a mother myself felt impossible. Pierre didn't help a lot—he said I looked grotesque and called me "Truck" because I was so big.

I'd been having nightmares for months with horrific images of the women I had "helped" through labor when I was a nurse in Chup. I told Pierre I didn't want to have anything to do with the obstetrics in any Cambodian hospital. Cambodia had become a place where everything was for sale, even doctors' diplomas. He told me it was no problem; I could give birth in the Thai capital, Bangkok.

I flew to Bangkok for a routine visit two weeks before the birth date. Pierre's mother met me there. She was much nicer to me now, and eventually we would grow quite close. The hospital was very clean, very crisp, and very technical, but the whole visit didn't make me feel any better about having a child. I couldn't understand the doctor—he spoke only Thai and English, and in those days I didn't speak English.

The doctor told me my contractions had already begun. It was all over very quickly—I gave birth before Pierre even arrived. After it was over, they handed me the baby. The room was dark. I held this warm, beautiful little creature whose name we had already decided on. After much discussion, we had opened a dictionary and fallen upon the name of a Turkish town between Cambodia and France—Adana. She looked very peacefully into my eyes.

Something happened to me that night. It was almost like my life began again, a whole new life. This was my baby, my child, who'd come out of my body, like I came out of my mother's body, the mother I can't remember and never will. I looked at her all night long, crying, "My little baby, I don't want you to have a life like me." I told her, "I will never leave you," and promised that I would keep her safe.

We went back to Phnom Penh. My mother-in-law was enchanted by baby Adana. It seemed now that everything was forgiven because I had produced a grandchild. Pierre too was delighted. When we went for a walk with our little girls, Ning and Adana, he told me I was beautiful. I was happy.

When baby Adana was about a month old, an American man, Robert Deutsch, contacted me. He said it was urgent. Robert had a group called PADEK that worked with squatters—and he told me there was a woman with him who said her daughter had been sold into a brothel. She wanted her daughter back, and Robert thought perhaps I could help her.

The girl was about thirteen and her name was Srey. Her mother told me she suspected her sister-in-law's friend had sold her. I went back to the neighborhood where they lived, and it seemed this woman was suspect: she didn't work, but she sometimes had large sums of money, the neighbors said. And her brother was a policeman.

When I got home, I went over to the police station near my house and found Srena, the young policeman who'd registered me. I explained what we were up to and I asked him to keep an eye on this woman, to follow her around for a little while and keep his mouth shut about it. He agreed unreservedly—he was a very decent man, and the idea of a child in a brothel against her will sickened him.

Srena came back and told me he had watched the woman go to a brothel in Tuol Kok, right near my house. I told him to go back there the next day and pretend to be a client. He would ask if there were any new girls, and try to find out if one was called Srey. He did, and the *meebon* told him, "She's too sick to see clients right now."

I talked about it with Robert, and he said we should both go to the police. Srey's mother was just a poor woman, and the police would never do anything about her complaint if she acted alone. But if Robert and I made formal complaints on behalf of our legal organizations, the police might feel obligated to take action—that was our only hope of getting Srey out.

We made so much fuss that the police agreed to raid the brothel. I think they didn't want to lose face. In those days, not many policemen supported our work. Too many of them were involved in the sex trade themselves—they worked as brothel guards or came as clients. Many of them were even investors.

That first raid was a farce. There were half a dozen policemen, Robert, the girl's mother, and me. As we went in the front door, the pimps and most of the girls were already fleeing out the back. But Srey, the girl we had come for, was still inside. She was white as a sheet and sweating on a filthy little bed on the floor. She was feverish, almost unconscious. In the space of a few weeks, the pimps had addicted her to some kind of drug—methamphetamines, I think.

We took Srey to the police station to tell her story and file charges. She was pale; she could hardly stand. Then she left with her mother. I visited her the next day and got her some medicine. But she was going through withdrawal, pissing on the floor, and it was clear her mother couldn't deal with her—she was trying to hide her from the neighbors. A few days later she asked me to take Srey—she didn't want her own daughter anymore.

Srey was the first victim who came to live with us. We had nowhere to take the girls and no money to set up a center, but we had two bedrooms and a living room. It wasn't large, but there was space enough.

In the beginning of 1996, Pierre, Eric, and I finalized our project to create a charity to fund a proper center to help prostitutes. We decided to call it something mild—we knew we had to avoid attracting a stigma to the girls who would be living there. We settled on AFESIP, which translates from French as: Acting for Women in Distressing Situations. This could mean anyone; it carried no label of prostitution.

We took our project to the European Community Hu-

manitarian Aid Office in Phnom Penh, looking for funds.
Three months later we still had had no response and when
we called the secretary said our papers couldn't be traced.
When we went back to submit the paperwork again, the EU
representative was there. She asked, "What is it that you actually want?"

We explained the project to her and she said, "But there
are no prostitutes in Cambodia." She had been in the
country for at least a year.

I'm not a diplomat. "Madam," I said, "you're living in
a world of air-conditioned hotels and offices. This isn't an
air-conditioned country. Go outdoors and take a look
around."

We didn't get any money from the EU. We didn't get any
money from anyone. All the big international organizations that were in Cambodia to fund grassroots projects like
ours knew about our mission, but helping prostitutes
didn't seem like a priority to them, and they weren't giving
us money. Sometimes, if a journalist wanted to write about
the traffic in sex slaves in Cambodia, these organizations
would send the reporter to me. But AFESIP was never
quoted in the article—the big organizations would take all
the credit.

Pierre's salary had once seemed princely, but his
monthly three-thousand-dollar paycheck was now completely absorbed by our daily needs and my work. I began
working for a real-estate agent, trying to make a little extra
money by finding houses for the foreigners who were now
flooding into Cambodia with nongovernmental aid organizations. What we needed was a lot more money—enough
to start up a proper center where former prostitutes could
live and learn to stand on their own two feet again. But at

least this new job would give me a little extra, enough to
fund the girls in our house and get them sewing instruc-
tion.

My job was to find houses for foreigners. I looked for
places with charm and with gardens—not the featureless
concrete villas that developers were slapping up all over
town. I understood what foreigners wanted, because in
some ways I was now partly foreign myself.

One afternoon I knocked on the door of a small house
that lay behind a beautiful Cambodian garden, with orchids
hanging in a banyan tree. An old man lived there. Renting
his house out was the last thing he wanted to do, but we
started talking anyway, and he asked me in for tea.

He was an intellectual and he'd been through every kind
of revolution and change and suffering too—it was marked
on his face. He said, "In Cambodia we're like frogs in front
of the king. When the king orders it, we poke our heads
above water and sing. When he signals, we go back into the
water. But if we poke our heads out without having been invited to, the king cuts them off with his sword.

"I've seen everything and lived everything," he told me.
"It's all useless. When you're young, as you are, you're en-
thusiastic. You want to understand a great many things. It's
no use. I fought all my life and for nothing; now I wait for
death. The only thing to hope for in this world is the peace
you need to look after your own garden."

I understood him and I thought about his words often.
When you're a frog, it's best to keep your head low. You
don't stick your neck out and try to change the world. I understand that. I don't feel like I can change the world. I
don't even try. I only want to change this small life that I see
standing in front of me, which is suffering. I want to

change this small real thing that is the destiny of one little girl. And then another, and another, because if I didn't, I wouldn't be able to live with myself or sleep at night.

In August 1996, a big conference on the sexual exploitation of children took place in Stockholm, Sweden, and several journalists wrote about the situation in Cambodia. After that, the big international aid agencies seemed more interested in our plans for AFESIP, and one big UN agency promised us funds.

They were a long time coming. By now, Pierre and I had several girls living with us. One was pregnant, two had been addicted to drugs by their pimps, and another had two children under the age of five. They all slept in our spare bedroom. Pierre and I slept with Adana and Ning in our room, and if there was too much crying from the baby, Pierre would try to catch some sleep on a cot in the corridor.

It was a lot to take, and Pierre was becoming exasperated. After a series of sleepless nights, he exploded with rage one day and told me that if we couldn't find a better solution, I would have to throw the girls out. In desperation, I went to Robert again. He talked to John Anderson at Save the Children UK, and they decided to lend us a house, which would become our first center.

It was a small wooden house on a tiny plot of land in northwest Phnom Penh. I could hardly believe our luck. At last we would have somewhere to house and feed the traumatized women and girls who so badly needed a refuge. To get started, Robert gave us six thousand dollars from PADEK funds.

We needed somebody to help run this place, to cook and

to live there, to keep it organized. We didn't have the money to pay a salary, and who would work for free? Then I thought of my adoptive mother. She looked after people. I knew that she too had once been in a brothel, even though we had never even broached the subject. I knew she would never look down on the girls in our care.

I went to Thlok Chhrov to talk to her about it. By the time I finished she had tears in her eyes and wordlessly began putting her clothes into a suitcase. Father was quite surprised by this. He had no plans to move to Phnom Penh, but he agreed that Mother should come back with me and work for a while at the new AFESIP shelter.

Our shelter began as just that—a shelter, a place of refuge. It was a one-room house on stilts, and everyone slept together on mats on the bare floor. Dietrich's friend Guillaume had given me ten sewing machines, but there was no room for them. We had to set them up on the bare earth underneath the house, exposed to the rain.

The sewing machines were crucial. My mother could teach the girls to cook, but they also needed a more marketable skill. A trained tailor who knew how to draw a pattern and fit a dress could make real money—honest money—and hold her head high.

But I couldn't afford to pay for a sewing teacher to train the girls. In Phnom Penh, tailors were now asking four hundred dollars a month to train one apprentice. Finally, after thinking about it for a long time, I asked Phanna if she would teach sewing. She had always been a good tailor, and she was used to teaching. She knew I couldn't pay her, but she wanted to move back to Phnom Penh anyway because she had learned that her husband was fooling around with other women.

We also hired a woman to do the accounts. She was the only one of us who was paid, and her salary was tiny, I think fifty dollars a month. We had enough money to pay for a few months of electricity, food, and medical treatment. For a long time, health care was our biggest expense.

We held an official opening ceremony on March 8, 1997—Women's Day. By then we were sheltering about twenty women. I was very nervous. I had invited my hero to the ceremony and I wasn't sure she would come. Men Sam An was the head of a government body called the Central Administration Commission, as well as a number of women's associations, and she was a fighter. During the Khmer Rouge years she was indoctrinated and enrolled in the militia like all the other young people, but she fled into the forest and became a guerrilla, fighting the Khmer Rouge. Later the Vietnamese-backed government made her a cabinet minister. Sometimes, when I was in Chup, I would see photographs of her in a newspaper—a small woman, pretty and smiling, wearing military fatigues.

Men Sam An came to the ceremony, with a whole entourage of staff and bodyguards. She was very simple and seemed genuinely interested in our work. She signed our guest book. When the time came for me to speak I was so overcome by emotion I could hardly talk. I really messed up my speech. But I was so proud. My two dreams were to open a women's shelter and to meet Men Sam An, and now both had come true.

Guardian Angels

I was still doing social work in the brothels, distributing condoms and health information and taking girls to clinics. This was useful work in itself, but it also served as a kind of cover, because I could encourage girls to escape and come to our shelter in secret.

I was also working with the police. I began informing them whenever I heard about a girl who had been sold or kidnapped and was being held under guard. We would pressure the police to stage a raid on the brothel, and then Pierre or I, representing AFESIP, would go along on the raid as observers. That way, the police would release the girl into the custody of AFESIP instead of taking her to a police cell.

But the whole process was often extremely difficult. The

police in Cambodia are not like policemen in the West. Especially in those days, many police officers were in the pocket of the pimps. Sometimes they took money from them in return for protection and sometimes they beat up clients who refused to pay. Some policemen even owned brothels, and many were regular clients.

Every so often we would come across a decent policeman—someone like Srena, who had compassion for the children who were being abducted and abused. Often these men were new to the force, with no power to change anything, but if a family came to the station to report a stolen daughter, they would alert me. Then I would dress up in my Khmer de France clothes and come to the station to file a formal complaint in the name of AFESIP, just like a white person would. That sometimes got the process moving, because it was more difficult to ignore.

By the end of 1996 we had about a dozen women living in the shelter. We had gone on perhaps a dozen police raids and saved girls who were chained and guarded in horrible conditions. Yet it was becoming difficult for me to go into the brothels as a social worker, because people had begun to recognize me. I was shoved around and threatened.

Meanwhile, good people were joining our effort. A woman I had known in Kratie had recently moved to Phnom Penh to work as a translator. Chang Meng was a woman of great intelligence and compassion who had suffered a great deal. Though we rarely talked about it, I knew that she had lost her husband and children under the Khmer Rouge. I asked her to join me as a social worker and investigator, working in the brothels together. She's still with AFESIP today.

In 1997 a French journalist, Claude Sampère, heard

about my work. He was in Cambodia filming a story about land mines for his program, *Envoyé Spécial*. I had a pretty low opinion of journalists in those days—I had spent days taking reporters through brothels in Phnom Penh, translating long and painful conversations for them, only to find that AFESIP was never quoted and only the most titillating details were used.

But Claude Sampère was different. He and his team got up at 6:00 a.m. to accompany us on our rounds. When he interviewed the girls in our little shelter about their lives, I saw him crying. I'd never seen anything like that.

One of the girls Sampère filmed was Sokha. She was from a refugee family. Her parents had tried to leave Cambodia for a better life, but they were sent to a refugee camp in Thailand that was run by the Khmer Rouge. When they came back to Cambodia, they had nothing. They were beggars in Phnom Penh when Sokha's stepfather raped her and then sold her to a brothel. She was nine years old, and by the time we rescued her from the brothel, she was twelve. It was very hard for her to talk to a man about what had happened to her, but Claude was very careful, very respectful.

Another girl Claude Sampère interviewed was Tom Dy. She was a girl I found in the road one afternoon, in a neighborhood south of the Royal Palace. She was dirty, with her hair clumped with mud, and frighteningly thin. People were throwing stones at her. Her head was bleeding, she had sarcomas on her skin from AIDS—she looked half dead. I thought she was about thirty or thirty-five. I asked the driver to stop and I put my arms around her and took her into the car.

The driver said, "Are you mad? She's filthy, she has lice, AIDS—don't touch her." He was disgusted by the smell. But I took her to our shelter and washed her myself—I didn't want anyone else to look after her. I tried to bring her to the hospital, but the nurses glared at her. She told me she was just seventeen.

I brought her back to the shelter and talked to Pierre. He used his contacts to get her tuberculosis medication and other expensive drugs. Every morning I washed Tom Dy and dressed her wounds with antiseptic. She told me she had been a prostitute since the age of nine. The pimps put her out on the street and threw stones at her when she became too sick to work. With our care, she put on weight and became like the chief of the whole center. Tom Dy was a naturally positive person and became an enormous help around the center—cooking and cleaning and bustling everyone along, looking after the younger girls if they didn't want to eat or became depressed.

Tom Dy told Claude that her dream was to work with AFESIP, to help the other girls. But she knew she wouldn't make it. She knew she had AIDS. I knew it too, of course, and I knew that it meant she was going to die, though I didn't care to think about it. Claude seemed deeply affected by their conversation.

He and his crew also accompanied us on a police raid. We were looking for the daughter of Mrs. Ly, a Vietnamese woman. Because she was Vietnamese, the police wouldn't help her—the Khmer hate the Vietnamese even more than they hate the Chinese, and anyway, she had no money. Mrs. Ly told us that her daughter Loan had left the village where they lived to become a waitress, but now she feared that she had been sold into prostitution. She had heard she was working in Svay Pak.

Because the police wouldn't help her, Mrs. Ly went to

Svay Pak herself. She walked around the street waving a small black-and-white photo of her fourteen-year-old daughter. One young man pointed to one of the brothels. She knocked, and the *meebon* threw her out.

After Mrs. Ly came to us, we went to the police to ask for an authorization for Claude Sampère's crew to film in Svay Pak. It was a Saturday, which was probably a mistake, because the police don't like to work on Saturdays. Also, it gave them plenty of time to warn the brothel owners. When we finally managed to get a permit for a raid on Monday evening, there was nobody at the brothel. No girls, no pimps. Svay Pak was clean.

Pierre and I were furious with the police, and we threatened to hold a press conference to expose their double-dealing. They rallied and arrested one of the brothel owners. Somehow, they forced him to confess where little Loan had been taken. But when we got there, that house was closed up—these people too had been forewarned. How were we to work with the police under these conditions?

Despite the locked door, we refused to leave. Finally we saw some girls coming out of another house down the street, trying to run away, which made sense—many of the brothels in Svay Pak are connected by tunnels. Loan was among the girls. She was in shock. When she saw her mother, they both wept. We filed charges at the police station.

Before they left, Claude's team gave Loan and her mother a little money, so they could go back to Vietnam. They traveled discreetly, without any passports—Mrs. Ly knew a place where they could sneak across the border. We were still new to these matters in those days, and there seemed no better way to do it.

I began receiving threats. Men would phone our house in the middle of the night and threaten me or my family if I didn't stay at home. I received letters that said, "Leave Phnom Penh or you will die." One day when I was in the neighborhood around the Central Market, a man drove alongside me on a big black motorbike, the kind we call dog bikes. He held a pistol against my side and said, "Leave. Because I won't kill you, but somebody else will."

I suppose he was a contract killer who had been hired to eliminate me, but for some reason, he didn't want to do it. Perhaps I had helped his sister or some other girl he knew. So he warned me instead.

I took that warning seriously. It felt different from the other threats. The cold, metal feel of the gun against my skin was very real. That evening, I locked the windows and doors. I began pacing around the house every night, waiting for the sounds of a gunman outside. I was most afraid for my family—for Ning and Adana. I didn't know what those people might do to my two little girls. I was becoming a little unhinged.

Pierre said it was time to take a break. He took me and the children to Laos, where he had friends who would lend me a house. He said it was just for a while, until the trouble blew over. In those days Cambodians couldn't travel easily, because they needed visas, which were almost impossible to get. But because I was married to a Frenchman, I was French and could therefore get a visa easily. I left the AFESIP shelter in the hands of my mother, and she and my adoptive father came to the airport to wave good-bye.

The night before I left I wrote a letter to the Cambodian

prime minister, Hun Sen. It was like throwing a needle into a pile of dried rice stalks, but I was angry and I needed to tell someone in authority. I said the traffickers had threatened to roast my baby like an ordinary chicken and that I should not be driven out of my country in fear of my life because I wanted to improve the lives of women who were being kept and traded as slaves.

The night we arrived in Laos, I had a dream. I saw my adoptive parents' house in Thlok Chhrov burning. I woke Pierre and told him, "We have to go home." He was irritated. He told me to stop behaving like a superstitious old Khmer witch. "Try to live in reality," he snapped. Still, he promised that when he got back to Cambodia, he would find out whether anything had happened.

My adoptive mother was at the airport when Pierre arrived, and he could see that she was distraught. He said, "What's going on—has the house burned down or something?" She started to cry. She said, "How do you know?"

The evening I left Phnom Penh, someone had gone to Thlok Chhrov and put gasoline all round the house where my adoptive parents lived. I suppose they assumed that if I wasn't in Phnom Penh, I had gone there for safety. Perhaps someone watched my car drive away from my house, with the children and the luggage, and figured that must be where we had fled.

It took just ten minutes for my parents' house and everything in it to burn to nothing. It was only made of dried leaves and bamboo. Because they had gone to the airport to see me off, my adoptive parents weren't inside. However, there was an elderly man there, looking after the house while my father was gone, because of course it didn't have a proper lock. The neighbors pulled him out of the blaze. He was hospitalized, and he never fully recovered.

I knew then that the threats against me were real. But I couldn't stop my work. I was in danger, but so were the thousands of girls in the brothels. I was safe in Laos, but they were not.

Then I received a response to my letter from the prime minister. A little black girl from a tiny village had written to the prime minister of the kingdom, and this man actually wrote back. Hun Sen wrote that the police were investigating the arson of my parents' house. He asked me to continue my work.

I felt proud to receive such an acknowledgment. It's true that although many Cambodian officials are shockingly corrupt, and some are simply evil, I have also received support for my work from certain people in the Cambodian government. Without them, none of what we do would be possible.

I decided to return to Phnom Penh. The holiday in Laos had done me good. It had calmed me down. I vowed to be more careful in the future and hired a driver who was a former policeman to be my bodyguard.

When Claude Sampère's program aired in 1998, he invited me to France to talk on the air about my work. Pierre and the children came along—little Ning, who was seven and a half, and Adana. Before we left, Tom Dy asked me not to go. She hung on to me and cried. She begged me, "Don't go. If you're not here, I'll die and I don't want to die without you."

She didn't seem very sick—in fact, she had just begun to put on weight. I told her she wasn't dying and that we wouldn't be gone for long. I promised to buy her a present. She asked for something pretty to wear in her hair.

Then the day before we left, Tom Dy was hospitalized. She had some kind of galloping infection and a high fever. When I took her to the hospital, she asked me if I loved her and cried in my arms. She kissed me and begged me again not to go.

I thought about her every day during our trip to Paris. Phone calls were expensive, and I had no news of her for two weeks. One afternoon Claude offered to take me out to find something for Tom Dy. We were in a department store when my phone rang: Tom Dy was dead. She died alone, in the hospital.

I raged and wept. This sweet teenage girl, who was sold by her parents into prostitution, who had been beaten and raped for years, had now died from her ill treatment at the hands of people who had no compassion, no human feeling for anyone but themselves.

There is nothing that can excuse the sex slave industry in Cambodia. I am no big thinker, but I think even Pol Pot cannot be seen as an excuse.

After Claude's program aired, congratulatory phone calls started coming in from everywhere. But in spite of the good press, the funding situation at AFESIP was becoming critical. Claude took me to see Emma Bonino, who was then the European commissioner for humanitarian affairs, running the European Union's massively wealthy aid agency, ECHO.

Emma Bonino was a world-class politician and she happened to be in Paris that week.

When we arrived at her Paris office, Emma Bonino was shouting into the phone—a blond Italian woman, tiny but with ferocious energy. I shrank back, but Claude said, "Don't worry. She's like that—she shouts. But her heart is in the right place."

Emma Bonino already knew about our work. She spoke to me briefly and made a couple more phone calls in Italian, furiously chain-smoking throughout. Then after barking orders at some underling, she turned to me again and put her arm around my shoulder. She said, "You'll be all right."

I was astonished by the energy that emanated from this small, smiling woman who could shout down the line and at the same time show me such kindness. She is a rock.

Of course that one visit wasn't the end of our struggle. We had to go to Brussels to talk to the bureaucrats in the European Commission. It was my first visit to Brussels, and Pierre came with me. We looked like scruffy refugees, dragging our luggage around in the rain. I didn't have a sweater and I was cold; I was wearing two pairs of socks in my cheap shoes, and my feet were bleeding.

The bureaucrats looked down on us with barely disguised disdain—me with my twisted shoes, Pierre with his lopsided grin, our worn suitcases in the corner. Apparently we didn't have proper appointments. We were shunted from office to office. Finally we managed to get a commitment of subsidies from the European Community Humanitarian Aid Office, but the funding stopped after a year or two—we never learned why.

12

The Prince of Asturias and the Village of Thlok Chhrov

When funds began coming in from the European Union and from UNICEF, the first thing we did was start building a new shelter about ten miles outside Phnom Penh. By this time we had more than thirty women and girls sleeping in one room, and AFESIP's wooden house in Phnom Penh was much too small. They were young, almost all of them under twenty-two, and some of them were children. They had very different levels of schooling—many of them couldn't read or write. They were also traumatized. They had nightmares and suffered from drug withdrawal. They were suicidal, depressed, mute, or uncontrollably angry.

We began building the new center in 1998, and planned to name it after Tom Dy. We wanted to put up a series of buildings on a piece of land AFESIP had bought, near a village about ten miles southwest of the city. I wanted to have a large covered room for the sewing classes and a separate room where a full-time schoolteacher could hold small classes in literacy and basic math, according to the girls' different educational levels. We planned several spacious bedrooms, each with room for ten women's mats, and separate cupboards for every person and her personal effects.

Then, in June 1998, while we were building the Tom Dy Center, I was awarded the Prince of Asturias Award. Pierre took the phone call. He told me that the heir to the throne of Spain had chosen me to receive a special award for promoting humanitarian values. Neither of us had ever heard of this prize and we had no idea how they had heard of us, but we quickly learned that it was an enormously prestigious award and carried with it the almost unimaginable sum of five million pesetas, about forty thousand dollars.

To collect the prize, we went to Spain, with five-year-old Adana. Ning was in school, and my adoptive mother looked after her while we were gone. We traveled first class, which I had never done before. We were treated like kings, even though we looked just as scruffy as ever. When we got to Oviedo, the capital of the Spanish principality of Asturias, we were told that I would be making a speech that night. I hadn't prepared anything and I've always been terrified by intellectuals and any well-dressed crowd.

We were welcomed into a grand reception hall where TV crews and photographers were waiting. The Prince of Spain introduced us. The beautiful African woman standing near me was Graça Machel, the wife of Nelson Mandela and a great woman in her own right. Behind me was Rigoberta Menchú, who had already won the Nobel Peace Prize for her work in Guatemala—even I had heard of her. Emma

Bonino was there too—she waved at me and sent me an en-
couraging smile. There were seven women who were receiving awards for their work to promote the rights of women
and children. I felt smaller and smaller.

I was so nervous I could barely understand what the prince
was saying, but what I heard was very moving. He talked about
the indifference of Western countries to the horrible cruelty
of life in other parts of the world, where there is such pitiless
abuse of women and children. When it was my turn to take
the stage, I closed my eyes and just began talking about the situation of women in Cambodia.

I talked about my own life and about the girls imprisoned in brothels as slaves. I talked about how badly they are
treated, the violence that they must endure. I talked about
the gentle smile of Cambodian girls, and how that smile
isn't genuine.

I had no idea I could talk in front of a crowd for that
long. When I finished there was thunderous applause. The
lights came on slowly and I could see that some of the people in the audience were crying. I felt exhausted, but I also
felt that I had achieved something important.

The next day was the prize-giving ceremony. All of us had
been asked to wear the traditional dress of our homelands,
and a crowd gathered in the street to watch our procession.
The Asturians were also wearing their traditional clothes. For
me, it was as if the world had turned upside down. In my uni-
verse I'm nothing, a mere woman who works for imprisoned,
penniless girls. Here I was being treated like a queen. I felt
like Cinderella, from Adana's French storybooks.

All seven of us moved forward, holding hands. There
was the roar of applause. Then we had to pay our respects
to the prince. I had been dreading this. I thought that

meant that we would have to get down on our knees and bow
our heads to the ground, like Cambodians have to do, to
show we are mere dust beneath the feet of royalty.

I don't like to kneel. I'm no longer a slave. I hope I will
never have to abase myself and go down on my knees in
front of anyone again—I've done that much too much.

But the prince arrived in front of me very simply and
said hello. He held out his hand for me to shake. He talked
to me naturally—he spoke in French. In Cambodia there is
a special archaic language in which the king is addressed and
no one speaks it outside the royal palace. But the Prince of
Spain was friendly and seemed sincerely interested in me.

Then I met his mother, Queen Sofia. She is a wonder-
ful woman, firm and caring, and truly dedicated to the
cause of helping women around the world. Emma Bonino
translated for us. The queen picked up Adana and played
with her. I could sense that she was kind and good and I
liked her immediately.

I was fascinated by the casual charm of this amazing
family. These people were the monarchs of a powerful
country, and yet they behaved as though I was their equal. I
felt that I had spoken from deep inside me. They knew what
I had done, and what had been done to me, and yet they respected me anyway—a little Phnong girl, a dirty prostitute.

Afterward we were asked to sign autographs, and there
were photographers and a huge banquet with a crowd of
people. My feet were bleeding from the high-heeled shoes
I had bought for the occasion. I wasn't used to high heels,
so I surreptitiously stashed them in my bag. I spent the rest
of the evening shaking hands, dazed and barefoot.

The warm welcome of the Spanish made me think for the first time that our campaign had found real support and that we would no longer have to go begging. Until then, almost every time we'd gone to big Western donors for money, we were looked down at with cold superiority. The money came in dribbles, never when they said it would, and often less than we'd expected. But when I returned to Cambodia from Spain, I had enough money to undertake something really significant. But almost more importantly, I felt people finally understood what we were doing and how important it was to help us. I felt we were no longer alone. Until then, everything I had done had been spontaneous, instinctive, a little disorganized. Now I felt that AFESIP could begin to plan for the future.

After completing the Tom Dy Center, my first priority was to find a place where the children we had rescued could grow up. Some children could simply never be returned to their families—there was too great a risk that they would be sold back into prostitution. By now we were housing several very young children, some as young as seven or eight, whom we had rescued from brothels. These girls had suffered enormously and they needed care. They needed someone to talk to and trust. They needed to go to school and rebuild themselves as people. I didn't want to give them to an institutional orphanage where they would be rejected and mocked or merely fed and watered.

I thought the ideal situation for these girls would be to grow up somewhere outside Phnom Penh. Sometimes the pimps stood outside our shelter in Tuol Kok and threatened the girls. Its location was becoming known, and there was a lot of movement, with new women arriving and residents leaving all the time. It was not a stable place to grow up. The idea came to me that I could buy some land in Thlok Chhrov, near my father's property, and make it into a children's center. I had visited my father several times, and the village was growing—prosperity was spreading there too. The school was spacious. The forest was close. There were a lot of new people in Thlok Chhrov, and the old ones were excessively nice to me now that I was a white man's wife and drove there from the city in a car.

I wanted to show those villagers that even if you have been a prostitute, even if your skin is dark, you can still be a good person. You can be clever, and you can succeed. After the way they had treated me, I had made a good life for myself. I was helping others, and they could do that too.

Above all, if I built a shelter in Thlok Chhrov, it would be far enough from Phnom Penh that the children would be safe. They could grow up in a garden, straight and strong, and go to school.

With the money from the Prince of Asturias Award, AFESIP bought a piece of land right near the village school in Thlok Chhrov. As a matter of fact, the land we bought was the same field where I had thrown a grenade and practiced cleaning a gun in military training. All around it were rice paddies and orchards. On it we built a spacious house on stilts. It has a fishpond and a chicken coop and space to house a dozen weaving looms and sewing machines, so the girls can learn a trade. I want it to be beautiful for them too, so we plant flowers together. A seed is like a little girl: it can look small and worthless, but if you treat it well then it will grow beautiful.

Whenever we find underage children in the brothels, we always ask them if they want to see their families again. They are sometimes very young, but they deserve to be heard, and we do occasionally reintegrate girls back into their families, if their parents can be trusted. We need to be sure that they won't be resold, and we follow up such cases with frequent visits. Sometimes it is enough to give the family a little money, so they can start up a business.

But often the girls beg to stay on with us, and I take them to Thlok Chhrov. They see the little girls their age—seven, eleven, thirteen—in their blue skirts and white shirts, happy together. They see the food—it is good home cooking, and many of these girls are hungry. They see animals and flowers. They know that all the girls in our house have done the same things they have done, lived through the same life they did. They ask me, "If I stay here for a week, and try to go to school, can I have a school uniform like the others?" I tell them yes, and at the end of the week they want to stay forever. They can live with us, but only until they grow up. Then, as hard as it is to say good-bye to a child you have brought up—for whom you are, in some sense, her only family—it is time for her to leave too.

When the children moved into that center in 1999, my heart lifted. I felt that I had finally done something right. They live there in an atmosphere of love and understanding and they know they are safe. We have fifty-five children there now, and we recently expanded the house again. The youngest is Ath, thirteen months old. Strictly speaking, we shouldn't have taken him in, but someone left him in the garbage outside our center in Phnom Penh when he was a few days old, and the cook adopted him.

One of the girls living in our Thlok Chhrov house right

now is Sry Mach. She was six years old when AFESIP rescued her from a brothel, along with her sister, Sry Mouch,
who was nine. That was in early 2006. The raid took place
in a town near the Thai border and rescued about ten girls,
but those two sisters were by far the youngest prostitutes on
sale. We took all ten girls back to Phnom Penh with us, but
those two I took with me, on my lap. They were much too
frightened to talk. They didn't answer my questions and
only ate fruit like savages when I stopped by the roadside to
buy them some food. They held each other like little animals. They reminded me of little birds, with huge eyes and
with their mouths open only for food.

As I said earlier, younger girls are very likely to become
infected with HIV and other diseases, because of tearing.
Sry Mach has AIDS. She's very sick—she has had pneumonia
and TB, and she has been in the hospital several times. She
does not want to leave us to go to a special AIDS charity, so
she's receiving antiretroviral treatment from Médecins Sans
Frontières. She has never told me much about her story,
only that a white man hurt her. The AFESIP psychologist
says Sry Mach has put her trauma behind her and we should
help it stay that way, so we don't ask her questions. Her sister, Sry Mouch, is ten years old now and she's doing fine.

Another six-year-old whom we rescued recently is called
Moteta. After being alerted about her by another prostitute,
one of our informers—whom we call peer educators—we
found Moteta, beaten black and blue, in a cage in a Tuol
Kok brothel. She was sold to the brothel by her mother, and
almost immediately after, the *meebon*'s business began going
bad. The *meebon* called a fortune-teller, and the fortune-
teller said Moteta had brought an evil spirit. To get rid of it

they would have to hurt her, to beat it out. They had already sold her virginity, of course, but they put Moteta in a cage and beat her.

With children this young, you don't ask questions. Moteta calls me "Grandmother," and I tell her, "Don't be frightened, I'll protect you." I promise her that nobody will ever hurt her again. She's so used to working all the time that she's always trying to wash everyone's clothes and clean the house in the Thlok Chhrov center. She was in the brothel for so long that she called the *meebon* her mother. She's been with us for eighteen months; she's now seven years old.

Our oldest resident in Thlok Chhrov is Ma Li—she's nineteen, but she's lived with us ever since she was rescued, four years ago, and she doesn't feel ready to leave yet. She has her school certificate, but she wants to stay and teach weaving, and she's in charge of all the little girls now.

Setting up the AFESIP children's center in Thlok Chhrov is the best thing I have ever done. Most of the girls who live there are between twelve and fifteen years old, and they are so sweet to one another. The older girls call the littlest ones "younger sister," and when new girls come in they help them as much as they can. We have a nurse and we look after them. They go to the village school in crisp school uniforms. They can talk to a psychologist, but some of these girls don't want to talk. Weaving is another kind of therapy, a way of clearing your mind and making something beautiful.

They are good girls and look after the elderly in the village. They're always very respectful of adults and they're always first in the class at school. At first the villagers rejected them for what they'd done, because they were dirty. They called them whores. But now they admire them and protect them from strangers. They tell me, "Somaly, you bring up your girls so beautifully."

I tell the children I love them; I say they are good. I tell them, "It's up to you to show that, no matter what has happened to you, you are still clever and good and strong."

I know the people who paid money to hurt these children. I know the clients. Some of them are tourists, but most are Cambodians. They are *tuk-tuk* drivers, cops, shopkeepers—ordinary men. The only difference in social class is the order in which they use the girls. The richest, the government officials and big businessmen, go first. In the end, when a girl costs only five thousand riel—just over one U.S. dollar—it's the poor's turn. It's hard to say which is worse.

To me, few people are lower than the men who use prostitutes. They pay to rape women, teenagers, and little girls. They use violence—they hit, slap, and bite, like in the porn videos that are on sale everywhere. It excites them to use power and to see pain. Although some clients pretend to believe that they are somehow doing the girls a favor, the reality is violence and rape. I spent a lot of time thinking about why, in Cambodia, people felt justified in treating women and children this way.

How do you become somebody who can be so careless about other people? Cambodians have been traumatized by the years of war and suffering, and it has made many people completely self-centered, especially in the cities. If there's an accident on the road, they won't stop and help.

The idea is, if you stop, someone may accuse you of having caused the accident, and you'll be stuck with the bill. And it's true—people do that.

To men, women are like servants. That's the way it has always been in Cambodia. Girls are taught only shame and ignorance about their bodies, and men have their first sexual experience in brothels. Rape is the only thing they know.

I wanted to try to begin to change this mentality. In 1999, Emma Bonino managed to get us funds for a campaign to educate men. We went to the Ministry of Defense to explain why this was essential, and we received the authorization to go to police stations and military camps and give lectures. The first time I did it, everyone said, "What? You're going to talk to them about sex? Aren't you embarrassed and ashamed?" I was definitely embarrassed, but I didn't think anyone else would do it.

I took Mr. Chheng, a male social worker from AFESIP, with me. We started off by explaining how to protect yourself from contracting AIDS. The men were interested because the epidemic was becoming widespread, and they were scared. We explained everything, starting from the very basics. With the help of a banana, we even showed them how to put on condoms. This was the moment to say things loud and clear, to get them talking. By asking them questions, we arrived at the problem of their relationship with their wives.

A lot of Cambodian men say they go to brothels because their wives don't like making love. They talk about this openly. Cambodian women are taught to submit, but the idea of female pleasure in our culture is foreign. The men say their wives' passivity disgusts them. No one is happy in this situation. Tradition says the wife must stay quiet, un-moving, while the husband gets on with his business.

One man said his wife actually told him to go to prosti-tutes. He never saw her naked and never even saw her breasts when she breast-fed their children. If he tried to take off his clothes, she said, "If you want to do like in those films, go see the whores." He burst out laughing—"Oh those young Vietnamese girls, just freshly arrived—when they get undressed, what a marvel! They're plump, they have white skin, like young piglets!"

The AFESIP lecturers confronted these subjects simply and directly. We talked about mutual pleasure, and pain. We showed them a video of a little girl who recounted how she had been raped—exactly what had happened to her, and who had done it. Sometimes one or two of the girls from our shelter would come to talk about what had been done to them. The men in the audience would often break down and cry. Many of them had been clients of prostitutes just like these girls, but somehow it had never occurred to them to think about how the girls were being treated.

In the first month we received four hundred letters from men who had attended our lectures. In the two years that we did this, we reached thousands of men, most of them soldiers and policemen—men who needed to think about these things. We taught them about what the brothels are really like and how they work. It was also useful because we made a few friends in police stations, even though most of them were junior police officers.

It took enormous amounts of organization and energy rallying the public to come to our events, touring with the education team, and maintaining the cars on our terrible roads. And in 2000, after Emma Bonino resigned from

her job with the European Union, our funding from
ECHO stopped. We decided to wait for better days to start
the program up again.

At that time we were suddenly swamped by a huge arrival
of girls from two rescue operations. Almost all of them
asked to stay on at the shelter. It was a bad time to be caught
short of funds. We called a meeting of all AFESIP Cambodia personnel to work out what needed to be done. In the
end we all had to pool our salaries and everything we had
left over from essential expenses in order to feed the girls.

AFESIP's financial problems always come at the end of
the year. However many girls we predict will come, there are
always more. It's impossible to refuse them shelter or to
evict them. I could receive funding for five hundred girls—
we would still need more.

13

The year 2000 was a difficult, painful time for our family. At around the same time as AFESIP lost the European funding for our educational campaign, I had a miscarriage. I felt horribly guilty that I had not been more careful and rested as the doctors said I should. Also, Phanna's husband left her. He took off with another woman, with all of Phanna's savings. Phanna was still a volunteer with us, teaching sewing classes for free, but she had a part-time job with PADEK, also teaching sewing.

AFESIP took shape slowly, in fits and starts; it was never a planned progression. We grew as the need arose. We set up basic classes in reading and writing Khmer. We expanded our training programs to teach cooking, weaving, and hair-

dressing—skills that can quickly translate into jobs. We began teaching every one of our residents small-business
skills, things like how to keep accounts and run a shop.
Whatever they end up doing, it'll be important that they
learn to keep their own accounts.

My father began coming to our center more often. He
had moved to Phnom Penh to be with Mother. She was still
the cook and caretaker of our shelter, and Father volun-
teered to teach the girls to read and write.

It amused me to overhear him teaching girls the *chbap
srey*. He would assemble them in a circle under the shade of
a tree. After class he would tell them that the good parts
of the old code are the need for silence and privacy. But it
doesn't mean you should not defend yourself. That, he
said, you are permitted to do.

Father never spoke to the girls directly about prostitution, but he told them, "What you have learned, from experience, is worth much more than gold. If you have a
house it may burn down. Any kind of possession can be
lost, but your experience is yours forever. Keep it and find
a way to use it."

We had begun receiving funding from UNICEF, from the
Dutch network SKN, from the Spanish government and
the agency Manos Unidas. Our Tom Dy Center grew larger.
The sex business in Cambodia was becoming more and
more professional, and it was reaching out to a new market.

The temples of Angkor were drawing tourists. Every
night of the year, thousands of foreigners rented hotel
rooms in the town of Siem Reap, nearby. They were Japa-

nese, German, American, Australian—and some of them wanted to sleep with young girls and children. We began finding so many girls imprisoned in brothels in Siem Reap that in 2001 we opened a shelter there too. Until we intervened, the police had never done anything about it, because they had never been told to.

Most of the clients of Cambodian prostitutes are locals, but some are foreigners. It's a very profitable business, the sale of sex. The traffickers earn a lot of money, especially if the girl is young. In Siem Reap, an ordinary girl, not a virgin, might bring in about fifteen dollars for about five days of work. Four girls will make you almost $360 a month, and cost you nothing but a bit of rice and a few guns. Since the annual income of more than a third of the population is less than $360 a year, with profits like these it's clear that you can bribe whomever you want.

And it's not just Cambodia, by any means. Every day fresh girls are trucked from Cambodia across the Thai border. Cambodia is a destination country, a transit zone, a place of export; Cambodian girls go to Thailand, Vietnamese girls come to Cambodia. It's an industry whose product is young human flesh. With fake passports, the girls are sent to Taiwan, Malaysia, Canada. Mafias traffic women around the world. It's a huge global business, as lucrative as drugs, and Southeast Asia is one of its epicenters.

In 2002, I was in France, accepting an award from the town of Nantes, when I received a phone call. A group of armed policemen had come to our AFESIP shelter in Phnom Penh. We had recently taken in fourteen young Vietnamese

girls after a brothel raid. The girls had been brought to
Cambodia from Vietnam, and they had no passports. The
police arrested the girls for "immigration irregularities"
and took them away.

Of course, what really must have happened was that the
pimps paid a judge a lot of money to get the girls back.
Young Vietnamese girls are a prize in Cambodia for their
white, fresh skin. By the time we got a court order to release
them, most of the girls had already disappeared, and we
never saw them again.

If I had been there, if I had had a gun on me, I don't
know what I might have done. I felt real violence within me.
There is no law, no police, no justice to protect little worms
like us. If you're strong, or if you have powerful protectors,
you're left alone. If not, forget it.

After that happened, we set up an AFESIP office in
Vietnam and began talking to the Vietnamese and Cambodian authorities about setting up a safe way to get these girls
home. We proposed that the Cambodian police could release the girls into the care of AFESIP, at least until the
Vietnamese authorities could identify them. That would
keep the girls safe. We offered to help the police by identi-
fying the people who created the problem—the traffickers.
We also suggested that AFESIP could build a training center in Vietnam, like the Tom Dy Center in Phnom Penh.

The authorities agreed, and we made new, separate
arrangements for the Vietnamese girls we found. We rented
another house as a short-term shelter where they could
stay. Some of them spent only three months with us waiting
for their papers; others stayed much longer. We asked an
ethnic Vietnamese woman from Cambodia to give them lit-

eracy classes and a Vietnamese-speaking former prostitute to give them counseling.*

We also set up a new organization, AFESIP Vietnam, and opened a shelter in Ho Chi Minh City. It works just as we do in Phnom Penh. Some girls have nowhere to go: they are homeless or have violent families. Often they have stepfathers who try to take advantage of them; almost always, there is rejection by their family or community. These days there are traders in almost every province—people who make a commission from the brothels when they bring in a new girl. It is better for our girls to learn a skill and stay out of harm's way.

In 2001, I became pregnant again, and the doctor said the baby was a boy. Ning and Adana were over the moon about it. Ning was ten and Adana six, and both were ecstatic about having a baby brother. I tried to take better care of myself. I tried to travel less along the bumpy roads between provincial villages and stay in Phnom Penh a little more.

Nikolai was born in April 2002. The girls were adorable. They stayed with me in the hospital room in Bangkok that night, along with their new brother, and every time he whimpered they raced over to his cot to tell him, "Hush, little brother," all night long.

By this time, AFESIP's operation in Cambodia had become much more sophisticated. We had set up teams of social workers, many of them former prostitutes, to go out every day, distributing condoms, telling girls how to get to

*In September 2006 we had to close that center for lack of funds.

our shelter, and advising them on how to calm clients who
are drunk or violent. They also collected information on
where the brothels were. We printed flyers with our phone
number. We created and expanded an AFESIP clinic where
women could come for free medical treatment.

We offered small sums of money to peer educators.
These are often former prostitutes who alert us when a girl
is very sick or when a minor child arrives in the brothels
from the countryside. Nowadays pimps change their "personnel" every two or three months in order to attract customers with the appeal of novelty. Then they trade the girls
on, to brothels in the countryside, or in Thailand.

We hired a psychologist to talk with the girls, because so
many of them are depressed and suicidal. We sent teams out
at night to the parks and open areas where some of the worst
kinds of prostitution take place. The "orange women" are
girls who sell oranges in the public gardens. For the price
of an orange, the client also fondles the girl. For twenty-
five cents he can have sex with her. Often a crowd of men
will gang-rape an orange girl, and it's not uncommon to
find a dead body in the morning.

These prostitutes don't have the money to pay for medical care, but they have our telephone number. They call us
when they're ill, and our *tuk-tuk* driver brings them to our
clinic. Here they can receive treatment and rest for fifteen
days or so, if they are able. We make use of the time to explain that there are ways out of their situation, that their
lives aren't over. When they understand this, hope can return to them. They may begin to believe that they are not
alone, that we can help. One day, they will come to us, but
until then, they help us by letting us know about children
and young girls who are being held against their will.

We cannot rescue every prostitute in every brothel. We try to focus on the worst cases, the captives, the children. When we hear about these things, we send investigators to the neighborhood. One of our full-time investigators is Srena, the young cop I met when I first moved back to Phnom Penh. They pose as clients. They talk to the girls in the brothels and take down their statements. If the girls say they have been sold, we make up a dossier and bring it to the government office of trafficking for evaluation, so that they can decide what needs to be done and verify all the details.

The local police are called in, but we try to withhold the exact location of the brothel until the last possible minute. AFESIP usually goes on the raid to observe the proceedings. We shelter the girls at the AFESIP center while a case can be prepared against the brothels.

I talk with every woman who comes into our center. I don't judge her, and she knows that. I sit beside her and explain that if you've been a prostitute, it doesn't mean your life is over. I talk about the women we employ, many of whom are former prostitutes too. I show these girls my clothes, and say, "You can learn to make this." I tell them, "Don't trust me, because you mustn't trust people. Decide for yourself."

In 2003, we opened an AFESIP garment workshop, and I take the women there. They know that in Cambodia a garment factory is often a brutal place, crowded and poorly ventilated. Many women are so ill treated and exploited there that they may even choose to become prostitutes voluntarily, though initially they don't usually realize what that choice means. Our AFESIP Fair Fashion workshop isn't like that. It's a decent environment, where every employee is treated humanely, and a girl knows that every woman who works there has shared her experience.

She can see that it's possible to get out of prostitution and make your way to a decent life that is clean. Almost all the women who come to us have some kind of illness or another. Sometimes it's just that they've been starved and beaten, but after ten or fifteen unprotected sex acts every day for weeks or years, you catch diseases. Many of them have tuberculosis or HIV, and they usually agree to stay with AFESIP, if only to rest for a few days.

If they leave, these women know they can come back. There's a wall around our shelter in Phnom Penh, but that's to keep the pimps out, not to keep the girls in. And if they stay with us, we give them a completely new environment. At the Tom Dy Center, a paralegal whom we work with gives each woman advice and explains her rights. These women usually have no idea about this—after all, there is nothing in daily life in Cambodia to indicate that they have any rights. The paralegal urges them to lodge a complaint with the police. This can be a very important step toward rebuilding themselves. These girls need to feel they are not bad, not guilty for what they have done.

If they want to talk, we have a Khmer psychologist on staff, and this therapy can help to free them of the burden of their oppression. But talking is not an easy or common thing in Cambodia. People tend to be very restrained, and tradition demands you remain silent about misfortune.

In 2003 we opened an AFESIP office in Thailand, where the prostitution and trafficking industry was even larger than in Cambodia. We began looking through the centers where the Thai authorities kept illegal immigrants. Many girls there were from Cambodia and Vietnam and had been taken across the border by force to become prostitutes. The centers were not safe for them, and we began helping them get back home. We also began participating in rescue operations in Thailand.

In 2006 we set up another office in Laos, with a shelter and training center in the Sisattanak district. A few years ago a survey by the International Labour Organization found that almost one in ten women and girls from Sisattanak had left home to go to Thailand. One-third of them were younger than twenty-five. These girls leave home with a trader, often a woman who tells them they will be hired as domestic servants. They become bodies on sale in the big glassed-in bars in Bangkok, where the world's tourists pick a girl by her number, or they service locals in other much dirtier and more violent places on the side of the road.

AFESIP's shelter in Laos gives them medical care and vocational training, so they can return to their villages or start a new life on their own. We teach the women to cultivate mulberry trees and to produce and market silk. There are so many girls that we'll soon need another shelter in Savannakhet Province. Eventually we need to start a shelter in Burma too, though it's difficult to get the authorities to agree; we see huge numbers of Burmese girls.

At Siem Reap, there's even a brothel with Korean, Romanian, and especially Moldovan women. The Asian clientele will pay a great deal for that kind of exoticism. It's a global industry, and for some reason the world puts up with it.

The advantage of this network of offices is that AFESIP can now act as a mediator between Vietnam, Laos, Cambodia, Thailand, Malaysia, and Singapore, to help them pool their efforts to protect these women, and to help these women return to their homes. Most important, we can give the authorities information so they can fight the traffickers.

In the years since we first set up AFESIP in Cambodia, we have helped more than five thousand victims of prostitution get back on their feet. In Thailand, Laos, and Vietnam we have helped another one thousand or so. All of them have to go back to normal life at some point, and they have to be equipped to look after themselves.

Reintegration can be a long process. It takes a year and a half to train a woman to take the test for the government's hairdressing certificate. If she has been badly damaged, it may take months for her to rebuild herself before she is even ready to begin. Some girls can become independent after ten months. For others who have suffered deeper trauma, it takes a minimum of two years.

When their training is over, we find every girl a job in an environment that is safe and humane, or we buy her the basics to set up an independent life—a sewing machine or a pig. We also visit her regularly, at least once a month for the first three months and repeatedly after that, for at least three years. That's the minimum time for assuring ourselves that our efforts have succeeded.

Some of the girls are like part of our family. They invite us to their weddings. After ten years, they still bring their children for a visit, every year.

We can do all of this only because governments and organizations give us money, but we also need the donors' support in much more important ways. To explain this, we always ask our benefactors to come and visit AFESIP. A few years ago, the Spanish secretary of state for foreign affairs, Mr. Cortés, came to see us with a government delegation, and they visited the sites. Mr. Cortés listened through an interpreter while a few of the girls told their stories. He came away transformed. He told me that he had heard me explain the work several times in Spain and that he had read the reports, but what he had heard here directly from the lips of the victims surpassed understanding. He was overwhelmed.

Sometimes it's hard to convince the donors to visit. They stay in their air-conditioned offices, push their paperwork around, and simply don't have the time. I try to tell them that their human presence and moral support are as important as their financial aid to the girls, who need to be recognized as full fellow human beings.

We have a great deal of support from many people around the world, and for that we are very grateful. But we sometimes have the impression that, for some benefactors, giving money is a way of getting rid of the problem—they don't want to hear any more about it. It goes without saying that we can't do this work alone. It's too big for us. We want our action to be part of a whole chain of action, because it is not enough to look after some of the victims: we want human trafficking to end.

14

The Victims

Since we started AFESIP, the brothels have grown larger and more violent. We find women chained to sewers. Girls come to us beaten half to death. They are so young. Increasingly we see that the *meebons* have addicted them to drugs so they won't ever try to escape. When I was young we were terrorized with snakes and heavy fists, but these girls suffer a more brutal sort of torture. They have marks that are worse than anything I have ever endured.

One day a girl named Srey Mom arrived at the shelter in Phnom Penh. She was bleeding and black and blue all over. I knew we should take her to the hospital, because I thought she might die from the wounds, but she begged us not to take her there—she said the pimps would go there to look for her. She pleaded, "If I die, let me die here."

We looked after her. When she got better, we started to talk. She was fifteen. She had been sold to a brothel run by a well-known pimp who caters mainly to the military police. This man is known to have killed several girls. Srey Mom was locked up there for four months, beaten, chained, raped without respite.

The house, which was in Tuol Kok, was built on stilts above a marsh, like so many Cambodian houses. The sewage ran directly into the water. One evening, Srey Mom made a hole in the floor big enough to slip through and she waded through the watery filth. She went to the police and told them everything. The police wrote down everything she said. They proposed to take her to a shelter on a motorbike. She gladly accepted. Then they took her back to the brothel from where she had just escaped.

The pimps thrashed her, and she thought they would kill her for sure. She made it out again, through the same hole, which was hidden. In the morning, having asked some people the way, she arrived at the AFESIP shelter, which wasn't far off. She didn't want to leave our shelter because she was certain the pimps and their friends the police would be patrolling the area. She didn't even trust the hospital—she knew that anyone could sell her for just a few dollars.

Srey Mom said one girl in her brothel was kept chained up. She said another girl had been tied up and burned because she refused clients and had tried to escape. Srey was certain she was destined for the same fate—a fate her grandmother had sealed when she sold her into this life.

A while back, I met a mother who would go to a brothel to get the money her ten-year-old daughter earned for her.

When I reproached her for this, she retorted, "She's my daughter. I carried her for nine months; I suffered to give birth to her. I'll do what I like. She's not yours."

"I have a daughter that I carried too," I objected. "I suffered as well in giving birth. But if I haven't got anything with which to feed my child, I'm the one who'll go out and prostitute myself, not her."

"Well, I have a husband who beats me. As soon as there's any money in the house, he drinks, then he beats me up and rapes me. He hits the children. And my daughter is in the brothel so that, thanks to her, there's a little money. And maybe she'll meet a man who'll marry her."

Another time we were talking to a man who had raped his own daughter, a mere child. We asked him why.

"Her mother is beautiful and she attracts all the cocks in the village. So to hurt her, I raped her daughter, who's pretty too."

"But this daughter is also yours!"

"No, she's her mother's. It's her mother who was pregnant. This child is nothing to me. I didn't carry her in my womb, did I?"

These are the kind of answers we get when we inquire.

Often, it must be said, parents don't know where their daughter works or exactly what she does. I think some parents truly believe that when they sell their daughters to traders, these men and women will find them domestic work as maids in the big city. But most of them do know their children are going into prostitution. To avoid paying commissions, they take their daughters to the brothels themselves. They know they are entering their daughter into a prostitution network that fans all over Cambodia, that trucks girls to Thailand, to Laos, to Singapore, even as far as

Canada. But these parents do it anyway. They care only about themselves.

Sokhon was the first child we had at AFESIP who died of AIDS. Her parents died when she was seven years old, and her older sister sold her into domestic service in Phnom Penh. The wife beat her and the husband raped her, and one morning when she was about eight she left the house where she was working and she walked as far as she could.

Sokhon ended up in the gardens in front of the Royal Palace, where a *motodup* driver started talking to her. He told her he would help her, then took her to a brothel in Tuol Pak, where she was sold, and raped, and tortured.

When we rescued her she was twelve. She had TB, along with AIDS, and was so close to death that her pimp just dumped her at the hospital. The hospital called us, because if they were going to treat her, someone was going to have to pay. I went to the hospital and found the money to pay for her care. She had every kind of mark on her body, and she was so thin she seemed made of rope. She looked like me, and her situation felt exactly like my own had once been. Everyone was frightened to touch her, but I took her in my arms.

I suppose some man paid a lot of money to have sex with Sokhon so he could purify himself of the AIDS infection. The belief that you can eliminate AIDS if you have sex with a virgin child is an abomination and responsible for enormous, terrible suffering.

Sokhon got better for a little while. She used to love her blue and white school uniform, but she knew she was going to die. That affected me enormously, and I spent a lot of time with her. She used to ask me whether there was a God and why he allowed such things to happen to a little girl who had never done anything wrong.

The first thing she asked me was to find and look after her little brother—that was what she was most concerned about. We found him and took him to a Buddhist pagoda; that was when I began asking a group of *bonzes* to look after the younger brothers of our girls and bring them up at the temple, since we can't house boys in our shelters.

Sokhon was very disturbed. One night, when she was already very sick, she asked me to sleep next to her. In the middle of the night, while I was sleeping, she cut my foot with a knife. She said she wanted to mix our blood—she rubbed her bleeding arm on me. She knew it could endanger me, and I think that she did it so she wouldn't be alone in her suffering.

Kolap was six years old when her mother sold her. When they got to the brothel, Kolap thought her job was only going to be washing up, but she pleaded with her mother not to leave her. She hugged her mother by the neck, and her mother slapped her and pushed her away. When Kolap grabbed her ankles, her mother kicked her. She walked away with fifty dollars, and Kolap's virginity was sold.

They scrubbed her down and plastered her with lightening cream, in order to make her a more appetizing color. When she resisted, they beat her for several days in succession. After her first week, they sewed her up again, without an anesthetic, and sold her to another brothel. She went from one brothel to another until she was ten, when we rescued her. Her life during those years was truly a journey through hell.

About a year after she came to us, Kolap asked me if I would take her to see her mother in Kandal. Before that she had always refused contact. I took her to her home village to find her mother. The woman actually started to cry when she saw her.

Kolap said, "Don't cry. I've come to ask you, why did you sell me? Why did you hit me when I kissed you? Why did you kick me when I tried to hold on to you? You had fifty dollars in your hands."

"I didn't sell you," stammered the woman. "I didn't know it was a brothel."

"How can you say that?"

"We had nothing to eat."

"You're lying. You've managed to live pretty well till now."

Kolap's little brother intervened to say he feared she would sell their younger sister too, only the child was hand-icapped and nobody wanted to buy her.

"You haven't changed. But you're no longer my mother. That's my mother," said Kolap, and pointed at me. "She didn't give birth to me, but she has given me all the rest."

We left. Kolap didn't want to stay for another minute in that house of sorrows. She was eight years old, with the body of a child, but her spirit was weighed down by an adult suffering.

Kolap is fourteen now, and she lives in our children's center in Thlok Chhrov. She's tall and she's at the top of her class in secondary school. She has never spoken of her mother again. She only says that as soon as she leaves us, she will bring her brother and sister to live with her and put them through school.

Sometimes parents take us to court to get their daughters back, with an eye to selling them on again. There's a profit to be made in it. But our legal position is strong—our charter authorizes us to shelter and represent such children. A mother who sells her daughter disqualifies herself as a guardian.

From time to time I am engulfed by rage at what I see around me. Recently there was the case of one young girl called Kaseng. Her parents were out one evening, and she was wandering in the streets when she was captured by a group of six or seven drunken men in their fifties. She was eight years old. They took her to a house and raped her one by one. Since she was too narrow, they took a knife and cut her vagina. Someone brought her to us. I took the child to the hospital to get her sewn up and then to the police to make a report. She began to recover. Her mother, who was very poor, said that ever since the child had been born she had brought nothing but bad luck, and she refused to take her back.

When the trial of Kaseng's abusers came up, an AFESIP staff member was sent to observe the proceedings. The rapists had paid off the judge. They claimed that she was provocatively dressed and that they'd paid her. In any case, they said, she was young and would have time to remake her life. The judge determined that it was impossible to send men of such venerable age to prison, and they were set free, laughing.

This child was a victim in every way—of the men, of the courts, of her family. We could have appealed the case, but she didn't want to. She pleaded with me not to do it. "I don't want to see them or hear what they're saying about me," she begged. "I never want to go to court again."

Blind with anger, I lashed out and told everything to a close adviser of the prime minister, a man who had helped me in other circumstances. I asked him to tell me how such a miscarriage of justice could be possible in a country that claims to be civilized. How can we allow our justice system to remain so corrupted by organized crime and by ordinary bribery that a crime as vile as this one goes unpunished?

My friend looked into it and referred the matter back to the court. We're still waiting to find out if the child can get some kind of compensation. But this can't work for every case—I can't telephone people in high places every time we lose in court, because sometimes it happens several times a month.

Even if we do make a scandal, the political authorities can only try to force the judicial machine into action. Then things get blocked up and nothing happens. The results are rarely satisfactory. We have laws in Cambodia, but everyone ignores them. The law of money prevails. With money you can buy a judge, a policeman—whatever you want. There are moments when I want to throw in the towel and stop doing all this. It feels too big for me to fight—the pimps, the corruption, the judges who aren't even for sale because they were bought long ago.

Corruption is like gangrene at the heart of the Cambodian legal system. All too often, justice is for sale. In the beginning, even when AFESIP managed to pressure the police into conducting a raid on a brothel, the pimps were often freed within days.

Since the start of AFESIP, we've brought about two thousand cases before the courts. We've only won about 5 percent of them, and most of those victories are recent. We know our way around the system now, and I think the judges are more careful these days: they know that AFESIP doesn't give up easily. Still, it's rare for the criminals to spend more than six months in prison, and most of them continue to be freed after just a few days in police custody.

Maybe it was different in Cambodia before Pol Pot. Even today, you do find good people in the countryside—villagers who care for one another and are always ready to share their meal with a stranger. But I was born after the great dislocations that ripped my country apart, and as soon as I opened my eyes on the world I saw only violence and corruption. Where are the supposedly admirable traditions of the Khmer? Where is their Buddhist morality?

I'm a Buddhist—just an ordinary Buddhist. I go to the temple sometimes. I give rice to feed the elderly at the village temple in Thlok Chhrov. But the men who torture girls also go to the temples. Are they Buddhists?

One day I put this question to the priest who heads the temple I frequent. He said, "Somaly, after thirty years of war, we even have monks who go to brothels and rape children. And there are others who are good and don't know why they're good."

I've spent a decade building AFESIP, and it's been a decade of pain. I can't distance myself from the suffering of these girls. We carry the same wounds. I share their suffering, their horrors. It is difficult for me not to blame all men for the actions of a few.

In those years of building AFESIP, Pierre had a lot to put up with. Our marriage was under a lot of strain, and it seemed not even the birth of our darling Nikolai could bring us closer together. In 2004 we separated, and we are now divorced.

In 2004, AFESIP began receiving reports about a hotel, the Chai Hour II. It was one of the biggest new brothels in Phnom Penh, a six-floor supermarket of female flesh, where customers could pick out girls standing behind a glass window, by their numbers, and have them delivered straight to their hotel room. Our investigators talked with girls who worked there, and they said they were forced into prostitution. Of the roughly two hundred girls working in the hotel as "hostesses" and "karaoke girls," many were minors. There were also virgins for sale on the premises.

To free these girls, we had no choice but to go to the police, even though we knew this wouldn't necessarily mean the guilty would be punished.

The Chai Hour II was a big operation—by far the largest brothel we had ever taken on. We knew that it was run by wealthy and powerful traffickers, and we realized that they probably had close connections with police and government officials.

Our dossier on the hotel was in the hands of the authorities by September. At the beginning of December, the police agreed to conduct a raid. An investigating magistrate had been designated as the person in charge. Once everything was decided, we had to move fast, since leaks were bound to occur.

The raid took place on the afternoon of December 7, 2004. Some of the people at the hotel managed to flee, but eight pimps were taken into police custody, along with eighty-three women and girls. There weren't enough police cells to house the girls, and many of them were underage. As usual, AFESIP agreed to take them into our shelter that night, to keep them safe while the police needed them for questioning, as several of the girls had agreed to bring charges against the pimps.

Before I left that night, I spoke to each of the girls. Some of them said they wanted to go back to work. One or two were the mistresses of highly placed men. For men of high position, there's almost an obligation to keep a little virgin or a minor in a luxurious brothel—it's a mark of status. (They usually also have wives and "official" mistresses with their own apartments.) These girls had expensive cell phones and used them to ring their protectors to express their outrage. I explained to them that AFESIP doesn't keep women against their will, but they had to stay with us under police authority. The police required them to be available for questioning for a few days, then they could leave.

Most of the girls were in shock. Several showed marks of their beatings. The youngest ones, especially, found it hard to comprehend that they were now safe—that they could stay with us if they wanted to and go to school.

When I left the AFESIP shelter that night, a large black Lexus was parked in front. Two men—two pimps—said they wanted to come in. We refused them access. Our rules forbid traffickers from coming onto our premises—that's why our Phnom Penh center has a high wall and a strong gate.

The next morning I began receiving phone calls. Well-placed friends called me, warning me to be cautious: "So-maly, you're dealing with important people here. You're going to get into trouble." The assistant of a person who worked with us in the anti-trafficking unit of the Ministry of the Interior called me in tears to say that her boss was in the office of the police chief, being fired.

I called another person I knew, and he said that he'd heard that the eight pimps had all been released. He too warned that I should be careful. He told me, "Stay out of this, it's too big for you." He told me I should free all the women from the Chai Hour II.

Then a woman who worked at the AFESIP shelter phoned to tell me that a mob of men was forming in front of the gates. She said that some of them were in uniform, from both the military and the police, and asked what they should do.

At 11:40 a.m. my contact at the Interior Ministry finally called me back. He said, "Release the girls. Your life is in danger. We have no power over this." At around noon, while I was still on the phone, about thirty armed men smashed down the gates. The girls and the AFESIP staff inside were terrified. They recognized some of the attackers as the eight men who had just been freed from jail. Their ringleader hit the staff members and threatened to kill them. The men forced all the girls they could find into cars or onto motorbikes that were waiting outside.

They took ninety-one girls in all, some of whom had been with us for only a few weeks and were beginning to

smile and trust that we could keep them safe. We never saw
any of them again.

One girl hid in the bathroom the whole time. She was
thirteen and had only come to us the week before. She had
just begun to believe that she really was safe now. When I got
to the AFESIP shelter and took her in my arms, she couldn't
stop sobbing and shaking.

I was angry, so horribly angry. What can you do when
the mafias that run the trade in women become so rich they
are more powerful than the law?

I phoned Pierre, who was in Laos. He phoned the
French embassy. Then a staff member from the AFESIP
shelter called. She said she had heard a group of boys in the
market saying they were going to lob grenades into the center and kill the staff one by one. I called a meeting and told
everyone we had to suspend our operations temporarily
and gave them all time off. I tried to help them stay calm,
but I was frightened too.

I am not an intellectual. I have no specific expertise. I
don't know how to speak properly and I've never had a
proper education. But sometimes it's up to me to stay calm,
to have an answer for everyone, to give people strength and
help them to overcome themselves. I live day by day, hour
by hour, minute by minute. I don't know what will happen
to me when I leave this room. Nobody does.

The next day, December 9, some of the local press began
reporting that the girls from the Chai Hour II had pushed
down the gate in an attempt to escape because AFESIP was
holding them against their will. They also reported that all
the girls were over eighteen. I began receiving countless

calls from people of influence in government and the police suggesting that I just keep quiet and not interfere in what didn't concern me. Friends warned me that I would get myself killed if I tried to make this into a confrontation and suggested I leave the country for a while, as soon as possible.

The municipal chief of police produced a communiqué that charged us with kidnapping the women and impeding the liberty of working people. It was a statement that was full of lies and venom. Journalists from local newspapers reported that the Chai Hour II was an ordinary hotel, offering massages and a karaoke parlor, and that all the girls were willing to testify that they were not prostitutes.

Pierre was flying home to Cambodia from Laos, but he called a press conference while he was in transit, in Bangkok, to try to get support for us from the international press.

The next day my children were followed by motorbikes on their way home from school. I knew I had to go to Kampong Cham, to check on the children in Thlok Chhrov. The staff who worked there were terrified that there would be a raid on them too, and the children were in a panic.

We left at four in the morning, but still, a car followed us. Fortunately they weren't very clever, and we managed to lose them before we reached Thlok Chhrov. I tried to calm the girls there. I told them that nothing would happen to anyone and that we had lawyers. I was trying to think clearly, but I was frightened too. I didn't want to take my friends' advice and leave the country—I couldn't simply get up and leave all these girls and AFESIP's staff behind.

But it seemed pressure was also building from an unexpected source. Officials from the American embassy came to see me, to find out what was going on and look into it themselves. We began receiving phone calls from people at the UN. I was invited to the French embassy to speak with the ambassador. Journalists began to call.

In the space of a few days, the tide began to turn. In Europe, newspapers were reporting the case, and we heard that diplomats from the European Union and the U.S. government were threatening Cambodia with economic sanctions if more was not done to stop sexual trafficking and corruption in the government. The Chai Hour II was now a symbol of something important.

The English-language *Cambodia Daily* led an investigation to see who had forced open the gates of the AFESIP shelter. Neighbors testified that it was the traffickers themselves who had led the assault. AFESIP received discreet invitations to return to work, and the government agreed to set up a panel to investigate the case and look into whether any corruption was involved.

Many months later, the commission reported that it "lacked evidence" of any corruption or that any women had been forcibly removed from the shelter. Some people are too big to take on. If I spelled out names there'd be a bullet through my head tomorrow. I'd have crossed the boundary that separates life and death in our country. That still may happen one day. But before it does, at least I will have spoken out.

In some ways, the Chai Hour II case unblocked the system for us. AFESIP began receiving markedly more help from the authorities. But eighteen months later, the Chai Hour II case came back to haunt us in the most horrible, personal way.

In July 2006, while a journalist, Mariane Pearl, was in Phnom Penh to interview me for *Glamour* magazine, Ning's school phoned. Ning had disappeared. She had left the school grounds at midday and hadn't come back. The cell phone I'd given her for her fourteenth birthday wasn't picking up. I instantly panicked. Ning is not the kind of girl who would just take off. She is a sweet, loving child. She has her own secrets, but she would never seek to worry me.

My instant reaction was that my deepest fear had been realized: the traffickers had taken my child. In Cambodia, this is not a far-fetched scenario. Every year thousands of girls are abducted and sold into prostitution. Most of them are poor, but my adopted daughter would be a special target. My blood froze.

I phoned Pierre, who was temporarily in Thailand. He promised to fly to Cambodia right away. Then I phoned everyone I knew at the police and in the government and told them what had happened. And I settled down to focus on finding Ning.

This is what I know how to do—I know how to trace girls through the prostitution networks. Every investigator we had ever employed at AFESIP went to see every informant who had ever contacted us. Very quickly, we heard that Ning had been seen getting into a car with several people in it, just outside her school. A woman and several men were in the car, and the woman was someone connected to the Chai Hour II.

Four days went by, of frantic phone calls and the even worse terror of waiting. During those four days, Mariane

Pearl was a rock for me. She told me about the abduction of her own husband, Daniel Pearl, by Islamic militants in Pakistan in 2002. She helped me retain my self-control.

I knew that if Ning had already been taken to Thailand, we might lose her. The first thing we did was send people out to the main border towns with her photo. Our only hope was if she was still in the country; in that case we might still find her and get her back.

Working closely with the police and the authorities, we finally tracked Ning down and, after three days, we were re-united. She had been in Battambang, in the hands of traf-fickers, along with a boy she knew. The boy had persuaded her that he was going to commit suicide over her, and she felt pity for him, so she had left the school to talk. Then he led my daughter to a car full of armed men.

I didn't realize Mariane would write about this incident, but she did. I'm sorry that my daughter's personal life has become a public story and I won't add to that. The people involved have been released from jail, although the trial is still pending. The Chai Hour II is still in business, still a brothel—it's called the Leang Hour now. And the woman in the car has never been found.

15

Conclusion

Today in our children's shelter in Kampong Cham Province we have a twelve-year-old girl with deep circular scars around her neck and upper arms from the time a drunken client tried to hurt her. One charming fourteen-year-old girl who has been living with us for almost a year has lost her mind. When we found her she was locked in the basement of a brothel, and for the first few months she was mute and couldn't control her body. Now she speaks, and she's learning to help out in the kitchen. She's very sweet, like a small child, but she doesn't always make sense. She wasn't always this way. We're still not sure who she is.

Sometimes I am flooded with anger at what these children have been through. I speak with some of the girls, and

I find myself overcome by having shared in their suffering. It eats away at my bones, until I feel almost deranged.

How did Cambodia get to be this way? Three decades of bombing, genocide, and starvation and now my country is in a state of moral bankruptcy. The Khmer no longer know who they are.

During the Khmer Rouge regime people detached themselves from any kind of human feeling, because feeling meant pain. They learned not to trust their neighbors, their friends, their family, their own children. To avoid going mad, they shrank to the smallest part of a human, which is "me." After the regime fell, they were silent, either because they had helped cause the suffering or because this is what they had learned to do in order to survive.

The Khmer Rouge eliminated everything that mattered to Cambodians. And after they fell, people no longer cared about anything except money. I suppose they want to give themselves some insurance in case of another catastrophe, even though the lesson of Pol Pot—if there is one—is that there is no insurance against catastrophe.

More than half the people in Cambodia today were born after the fall of the Khmer Rouge. Things should be improving. But the country is in a state of chaos where the only rule is every man for himself. The people in power don't always work for the common good. When I was young, we were poorer, but school was free in those days. Today, school has to be paid for, and you can buy a diploma—or get one for free, if you show your teacher a gun. The justice system is for sale, and the mafias are close to power; the prostitution business is worth $500 million a year, almost as much as the annual budget of the government.

Cambodian people have always been trained to obedience, and they have always been poor. In Cambodia, one child in eight dies before the age of five. The streets are full of garbage and flies and shit, and the rain churns it into muck. More than a third of the population lives on less than a dollar per day, and you have to pay the hospital when you get sick.

Men have the power. Not all the time; in front of their parents, they keep quiet. With the powerful, they must also stay silent and perhaps prostrate themselves. But once these encounters are over, they go home to assume the upper hand and give orders. If their wife resists, they hit her.

There is one law for women: silence before rape and silence after. We're taught when we're little to be like the silk-cotton tree: *dam kor*. Deaf and dumb. Blind too, if possible. Your daughters will look after you, because that's their duty. Other than that, they're not worth much.

One-third of the prostitutes in Phnom Penh are young children. These girls are sold and beaten and abused for some kind of pleasure. In the end I don't think there is any way you can explain or justify that, or the homeless children scrounging through garbage, inhaling glue from little cans you can buy for five hundred riels in every hardware stall, or the stolen children who are trucked into Thailand for the modern slave trade. Trying to explain it is not what I do. I keep my head down and try to help one girl after another. That is a big enough task.

I still feel that I'm dirty and that I carry bad luck. When I sleep, my dreams are filled with violence and rape. Most of my dreams are nightmares. Last night I dreamed again of serpents crawling into my trousers. I've tried to rid myself of these nightmares, but they continue to haunt me.

Consulting a psychologist isn't enough. I did that. I've tried a great many things. But the past is inscribed on my body now. When you see the marks on your skin, the scars of torture and cigarette burns, the shape of the chains on your ankles, you feel the past can never be wiped away. You carry the marks of the suffering. They're just there. But that's precisely why I carry on with the work of AFESIP.

A lot of people play a part in the work of saving children from sexual slavery, but I fear that some of the volunteers feel a sense of superiority toward prostituted women. They're contemptuous of them. For me, it's different. I'm one of them. Everything they've been through, I share. I wear their scars on my body and in my soul. We don't need to say much to understand one another. We know that life is a daily hell. Some of the workers here work for their salaries; in their hearts they don't understand.

When I close my eyes, I see the physical tortures again. I prefer them to the psychological ones, like the fear I felt when I was told my family and my collaborators would be killed. But even so, my eyes close and the blows and kicks are there. Remembering makes you want to die, but you're not allowed to die. You want to disappear, but you can't disappear.

The memories that torment me most are those of rape and the stink of sperm. In brothels, they don't bother changing sheets much. The smell of sperm is everywhere. It's insufferable. Even today, I often have the sense that I'm breathing in the smell of the whorehouses. The customers were dirty. They never showered. I remember one man with the most hideous breath. We had no toothpaste, but we would brush our teeth with ash or sand. Some of the clients never bothered at all; their teeth were yellow and rotting.

I lived amid this stench for so long that I can't bear it now. Even fifteen years later, I feel dirtied by it. So I wash myself like a madwoman, put cream on and cover myself in eau de toilette in order to mask the stench that pursues me. At home, I have a cupboard full of perfume. I spend money to blot out a smell that exists only in my imagination. I try to chase it away with the contents of my bottles.

Writing this book has brought everything back, and I can no longer sleep. It makes me sick. I have nightmares remembering all the horrors. Sometimes I don't know if I can bear to keep living with them. There are times when I'd like to get rid of this burden of memory that weighs me down, the roll call of my misery that forces me to have shower after shower, rubbing myself down as hard as possible before covering myself in cream and drowning myself in perfume. What's the use of such an existence? Apart from crying, what does one do with it? Are my friends who died and are now free of it all luckier than I am? I would have liked to live a happy life, but the problems are there, always in front of us, gaping, demanding our energy, our ceaseless activity, and even our despair. To say that the past is past, that you need to put it all behind you, is what I say all the time to the girls who come to the center with their unendurable suffering.

I know how to say all this, but I also know that it's useless and serves little purpose. Nothing can cauterize those old wounds. If I confide in Pierre or my close friends that I feel dirty, they tell me that it's not true, that for them I'm this, that, or the other, but I'm not dirty. These words

don't help me at all. The only people to whom I can say that
I feel dirty and who can understand are the girls who have
walked the same path as I have.

Journalists make it difficult, in a way, though I am very
grateful to them. The attention of the world's newspapers
helped save our operation from being shut down. But often reporters want a "sexy" project, something hot, to wake
up the readers and viewers. They ask me to talk about my
past—if not, how will they convey the importance of the
work we're doing?

That's one of the reasons I decided to write this book.
Perhaps it will stop me from having to tell my story over and
over again, because repeating it is very difficult. And one
day I may no longer be here, so I want everyone to know
now what is happening to the women of Cambodia. Given
what's going on in my country, who knows who may still be
alive tomorrow.

When we started doing our work, we couldn't manage to
close down the small brothels. We didn't have enough experience and the pimps and *meebons* just laughed at us. Then,
with time, work, and support, we began doing it. Now it's
the big brothels that pose the challenge.

We have to proceed step by step. We've been working for
ten years, but it's only in the last three years that we've begun cooperating well with the police. The justice system is
beginning to improve too. When there's an AFESIP case
these days, some of the judges are more careful, because
they know we don't let things drop easily. And some people
in government do help me; if we had no support from the
government, none of our work would be possible.

I never wanted to become a public person; it just happened that way. My dream, really, is to be like that old man who told me about the frogs and the king: I would like to have a quiet life, in a garden, living with all my children and with the girls from Thlok Chhrov. I would be a grandmother and great-grandmother and I would be happy, and someone else would have taken over the work of running everything. But so far it hasn't been like that.

I have written this book for several reasons. I want people to realize to what extent prostitutes are victimized and how important it is to help them. These women and girls are marked by their experiences for life, and it's very hard for them ever to find even a little happiness. It simply isn't true, as some people think, that the girls are glad to find work, that they volunteer for it, that they are well paid.

People think prostitutes are deceitful and dishonest. They think these girls are hard and intractable—we have a saying in Cambodia: "Don't try to bend the *sroleuw* tree, don't try to change a whore." On the contrary, prostitutes are often honest girls from the countryside, and most of them will do anything they can to leave the suffering they endure in the brothels.

My story isn't important. The point is not what happened to me. I write my story to shed light on the lives of so many thousands of other women. They have no voice, so let this one life stand for their stories.

On their behalf, I would like this book to serve as a call to the governments of the world to get involved in the battle against the sexual exploitation of women and children. Victims are victims in every country.

I recently set up a foundation in the United States that I hope will assist in our work. I want to be able to buy

enough land so that one day, the girls from our Thlok
Chhrov center, who have grown up with us, can farm it, all
together. AFESIP is about short-term help: we cannot support a girl indefinitely. We cannot pay to educate her beyond a certain level or allow her to stay on forever, even
though we may be her only family. Our new foundation will
provide longer-term support and it could help other
women—former prostitutes, but also orphans, ethnic mi-
norities, the elderly. We have called it the Somaly Mam
Foundation, because my notoriety helps us raise money,
but I hope the victims themselves will run it.

For the moment, our opponents are winning the war,
but we've won one battle at least. They've lost face and respect. We've investigated this traffic, exposed it for what it
is, and made it shameful. We've shown that these people
aren't invincible, and I'm glad we've managed that.

People ask me how I can bear to keep doing what I do.
I'll tell you. The evil that's been done to me is what propels
me on. Is there any other way to exorcise it?

Afterword

I feel stronger today than when I first wrote this book; 2008 was a year of discovery and hope for me. I was invited to visit cities all over the world, and everywhere, it seemed, I encountered people who listened to me with open hearts and clear eyes. Many became my friends and allies.

In Sweden, I received the World Children's Prize for the Rights of the Child. I am especially proud of this award because it came from children; six and a half million children around the world voted. How can I not feel stronger, knowing that these children are aware of what is happening halfway around the world and have given me their support?

In Germany, AFESIP was awarded the Roland Berger Award for Human Dignity. The prize came with a very generous—and much needed—financial contribution, but what I cherished most about this prize was its name. We have received awards and distinctions in the past for human rights work, but being given this distinction of dignity touched me like none before. When you are in the brothel, no one gives you any dignity.

In Washington, D.C., I was honored at the Vital Voices 2009 Global Leadership Awards, along with Hillary Clinton, Temituokpe Esisi from Nigeria, Sadiqa Basiri Saleem from Afghanistan, and Marceline Kongolo-Bicé and Chouchou Namegabe Nabintu from the Democratic Republic of the Congo. It was both a humbling and an inspiring experience. Vital Voices aims to identify, train, and empower women leaders around the world. It was very moving to share the stage with these powerful women and also to share our experiences together. There was a lot of focus on how women can act to improve our world, but I welcomed hearing the actor Ben Affleck state that men are responsible too: we share the world.

I am so grateful to have been given these opportunities to travel, to spread my message, to get the support and eyes of the world on Cambodia, and to try to convince world leaders that Cambodian women count. But when I'm far away I always miss the girls and women in our rescue centers. I worry about them. I can't wait to get back, to be with them and protect them from harm.

We've faced some difficult times this past year. For example, when I first wrote this book, Kolap was doing well in school and adjusting to life in our center. She kept the promise she made to her little sister and returned to bring her back to the shelter. But her mother became angry with Kolap and told her she was stealing her daughter—her source of income. Even in the most caring environment, sometimes the old ways and patterns are intractable. Kolap ended up leaving the shelter; she ran away, without telling us of her plans, and went to work in a factory. It took us months to find her, and when I think of the conditions she was living in, it makes me sick and angry at this mother who would manipulate her daughter and sacrifice her future for her own gain.

Kolap has chosen to return to us; she and her sister are safe, and she's training to work with other victims. She's more mature. I'm so proud of her. Sometimes you can learn, even from a bad experience; by coping, you become stronger. The pain does not go away, but it becomes manageable. Kolap is learning from her experiences. She's becoming a woman.

The Somaly Mam Foundation has made it its mission to give victims and survivors of sexual trafficking a voice. We try to rescue them, to help them create and sustain lives of dignity—like Kolap, who will soon be working to save other girls like her. Our goal is to put an end to slavery, to help create a world where women and children are safe from sexual trafficking.

I would like to thank everyone who supports us and other groups like ours. We count on you. We work in isolation most of the time and it can be very dangerous and discouraging. Knowing that you care gives us strength, courage, and the comforting knowledge that we are not alone. I strongly believe that love is the answer and that it can mend even the deepest unseen wounds. Love can heal, love can console, love can strengthen, and yes, love can make change.

Acknowledgments

I would like to thank all the victims for their courage and the confidence and trust they have given me. I love them like my own children and am so very proud of them.

I have a special debt of gratitude to all the people who have assisted in my work and who have helped me and AFESIP in our fight against sexual slavery. I am deeply moved by the humanity, warmth, and generosity they have shown for our cause.

There are so many special people around the world to thank; the list is too long to mention everyone, but I would like them to know that I hold them in my heart. There are some people in particular whose support has been vital. Emma Bonino reached out a helping hand when we were just starting out. Queen Sofia of Spain has been unyielding in her compassion and, from our very first encounter, has given me hope for a new life. The LexisNexis corporation, with their global commitment to the rule of law and human rights, has been an inspiration, especially Andy Prozes, Robert Rigby-Hall, and Bill Livermore, whom I trust and respect like a brother.

I am so grateful to everyone at *Glamour*, especially Cindi Leive and Mariane Pearl, for their friendship and support. My heartfelt thanks to Vital Voices and in particular Alyse Nelson Bloom. I'd also like to thank Susan Sarandon, Barbara Walters, Queen Latifah, Petra Nemcova, Daryl Hannah, Nicholas Kristof, Ayaan Hirsi Ali, Diane von Furstenberg, Norman Jean Roy and Jojo, Michael Angelo, Kerry Girvin, Jack Milon, Alice Kendall, Ernesto Carlos Gerardo, the Lumpp family, Renée and Anne Daurelle, and Catherine and her two daughters in Paris. Despite everyone's busy lives, they have given so much of their time, their hearts, and their energy. Thank you.

Thanks to Nic Lumpp and Jared Greenberg for creating the Somaly Mam Foundation and to all the members of the board who have been tireless in their hard work to raise awareness in the United States. They have proven that dedication and sheer will can bring about enormous change.

The Cambodian government went above and beyond to bring my daughter back to me. I am eternally in your debt.

I would also like to thank the people who have helped this book happen: Katrin Hodapp, my little sister; Alain Carrière, my French publisher, whom I view as an adopted grandfather; Ruth Marshall, who gave me the confidence I needed to find these words; and Susanna Lea, whose passion for women's causes I greatly admire.

Special love to my beautiful sisters, Chenda Sophea

and Ouk Vongvathany, and to my dearest friends Kimleng, Chantha, Kien Sereyphal, Sapor, Sofia, and Emmanuel Colineau for your spirit, kindness, and care. You have been a constant source of comfort in dark times.

I wish to thank my adoptive family, who took me into their hearts and taught me the values of silence, honesty, and hard work.

And to Pierre, thank you for saving me. I will always respect you and am so thankful that you are the father of my beautiful children.

Above all, I wish to thank my three children for their patience and for teaching me how to love.

Appendix

**A portion of the proceeds from this book will be
donated to the Somaly Mam Foundation.**

The Somaly Mam Foundation is a 501c3 nonprofit charity
that combats illegal trafficking and sexual slavery by sup-
porting organizations that rescue, rehabilitate, and reintegrate young victims. All organizations funded by the Somaly
Mam Foundation are audited operationally and financially.
AFESIP Cambodia is currently the foundation's primary
beneficiary. Led by Somaly Mam, the Somaly Mam Foundation is committed to ending sexual slavery and giving victims
a chance at a new life.

**To learn more about the Somaly Mam Foundation,
get involved, or make a donation, visit the Web site:
www.somaly.org.**

The Road of Lost Innocence

SOMALY MAM

A READER'S GUIDE

Reading Group Questions and Topics for Discussion

1. The theme of silence—both cultural and personal—runs throughout Somaly Mam's story. "People learned from [the years under Pol Pot] that they couldn't trust anyone—friends, neighbors, not even their family," Mam writes. "The more you let people know about yourself—the more you speak—the more you expose yourself to danger. It was important to see, not to hear, not to know anything about what was happening. This is a very Cambodian attitude toward life" (p. 14). Indeed, in this context, the fact that Somaly Mam, a Cambodian woman, wrote a memoir is itself an act of courage and defiance. What helped Somaly to find her voice in a culture that suppresses the cries of the individual? By what methods does she combat this conspiracy of silence?

2. Compare the Cambodian tradition of silent forbearance in the face of unthinkable adversity with the explicit repression found in political regimes that do not permit free

speech and individual expression. Which do you think is a more insidious and dangerous form of repression?

3.   In chapter 10, "New Beginnings," Somaly returns to Phnom Penh as a married woman and encounters an old man who lives in a small house with a beautiful, orchid-filled garden. He was "an intellectual and he'd been through every kind of revolution and change and suffering too." He tells Somaly, "In Cambodia we're like frogs in front of the king. When the king orders it, we poke our heads above water and sing . . . But if we poke our heads out without having been invited to, the king cuts them off with his sword. I've seen everything and lived every-thing . . . It's all useless. When you're young . . . you want to understand a great many things. It's no use. I fought all my life and for nothing; now I wait for death. The only thing to hope for in this world is the peace you need to look after your own garden" (p. 128). Somaly writes that she understood him and thought about his words often, but, she says, "I don't feel like I can change the world . . . I only want to change this small life that I see standing in front of me, which is suffering. I want to change this small real thing that is the destiny of one little girl. And then another, and another, because if I didn't, I wouldn't be able to live with myself or sleep at night" (pp. 128–29). Compare Somaly's life experience with the old man's. Somaly reached adulthood without a formal education, while this man is described as an intellectual who has seen and experienced much. What do you think accounts for their different views of personal responsibility, when arguably, a person such as So-maly, who has experienced and witnessed the most violent and depraved acts of man, has a greater right to feel self-protective and hopeless about humanity? Why does the old man advise keeping one's head low and tending one's garden, while Somaly risks everything to save one little girl's life?

4. Somaly writes about the status of women in Cambodia and their sense of self-worth: "There is one law for women: silence . . . We're taught when we're little to be like the silk-cotton tree: *dam kor*. Deaf and dumb. Blind too, if possible. Your daughters will look after you, because that's their duty. Other than that, they're not worth much" (p. 185). From a young age, girls are taught service and submission. They learn to expect violence instead of tenderness from men. Even Somaly, when she writes about her husband, Pierre, the father of her children, speaks with a frank pragmatism about her marriage: "I may not have loved Pierre, but I thought I could live with this man. He was simple, like a Cambodian. He ate rice and *prahoc* sauce . . . Pierre wasn't rich, but of all the people I had ever met, he was the only one who was attentive to *me*—not to my body, but to me" (p. 76). Her marriage ended in 2004, shortly after the birth of her son. Do you think Somaly's sense of self-worth played a role in the demise of her marriage?

5. When Somaly was carrying her first child, she confides, "I felt paralyzed by the thought of being a mother to someone. I had never had a mother and I painfully felt that hole in my life. To be a mother myself felt impossible" (p. 123). And yet, after giving birth, Somaly's fear instantly dissipates. "Something happened to me that night. It was almost like my life began again, a whole new life" (p. 124). What do you think Somaly felt after giving birth that transformed her into a mother? How do you think she finds the tenderness and compassion within to become the mother to those she rescues when also confronted with the most grim and desperate view of humanity?

6. In the chapter entitled "The Victims," Somaly writes, "Most [Cambodian parents] do know their children are going into prostitution. To avoid paying commissions, they take their daughters to the brothels themselves . . . But these parents do it

anyway. They care only about themselves" (pp. 168–69). Is it possible to understand the actions of these parents and find compassion for them in view of the mass trauma and psychic scarring Cambodians suffered during the many years of war and dictatorship that ravaged the country?

7.   In Nicholas D. Kristof's foreword, he describes Somaly as "the Harriet Tubman of Southeast Asia's brothels, repeatedly rescuing those left behind." Compare Somaly's brand of activism and confrontational style with that of Tubman's Underground Railroad. Which is the greater scourge—the ignorance and prejudice that allowed slavery to proliferate in the United States until the mid-nineteenth century or the cultural acceptance and capital that makes human trafficking one of the largest criminal industries in the world today? What forces must an antislavery activist of today confront that were not in place in the nineteenth century? What tools does Somaly have in her arsenal that Tubman did not? Whose challenge is greater?

8.   Arguably, when people act inhumanely they rely on a community of people who make excuses for their actions, demonize and disassociate from victims, deny wrongdoing, and look the other way when they are confronted with the truth. The very forces that are meant to provide safety—most notably the government, policemen, religious leaders, and parents—work in concert, either knowingly complicit or unwittingly, to foster this dangerous climate in Cambodia and other Asian countries where sexual slavery proliferates. And yet, human trafficking is not confined to Asia and the developing world. In fact, in a *Newsweek* editorial, the actor and activist Emma Thompson reveals that sexual slavery is prevalent in most Western countries, including the United States and the very section of London where she was raised. "Some 120 nations are routinely plundered by traffickers for their human raw materials, and more

than 130 countries are known as destinations for their victims."
What do you think we can do as individuals to combat this issue,
both at home and abroad?

9.   Why is it important to tell stories? Can you think of
other true-life stories that had the effect of changing cultural
attitudes? What books can you think of that have had an impact
on society in the time they were published and served as agents
of change? Do you think Somaly Mam's memoir has the power
to effect change on a global scale?

10.   In his foreword Kristof writes that Somaly's "is a
hopeful story. She may describe killings and torture, but the
larger story is of triumph, love, and rehabilitation." How does
a story like Somaly's, full of such unfathomable sadness, inspire
hope? How has the experience of reading her story changed
you?

11.   Ayaan Hirsi Ali writes in her introduction, "Somaly
Mam is my candidate for the Nobel Peace Prize. She is living
proof that one woman *can* change the fate of others." Past
recipients of the Nobel Peace Prize include Dr. Martin Luther
King, Jr., Mother Teresa, His Holiness the Fourteenth Dalai
Lama, and Archbishop Desmond Tutu. Do you think Somaly's
struggles and achievements are on par with those of these
winners?

SOMALY MAM is cofounder and president of AFESIP (Acting for Women in Distressing Situations) in Cambodia and president of the Somaly Mam Foundation in the United States. Under her leadership, the two organizations seek to save, rehabilitate, and socially reintegrate victims of sexual slavery in Southeast Asia and have rescued more than five thousand women and children to date. In 2006, Mam was named a CNN Hero and a *Glamour* Woman of the Year. She received the World Children's Prize for the Rights of the Child and the Roland Berger Award for Human Dignity in 2008, and in 2009 she was named to *Time* magazine's list of the one hundred most influential people in the world. She lives in Cambodia.